In 1986, after a stint as a burger flipper at McDonald's and a few years as a roof plumber, Rusty moved to Melbourne from his native Queensland to pursue his dream of becoming a bass player in a rock band. Something got mixed up, because three months later, he was in a barbershop quartet playing festivals and shopping centres around Melbourne. After a two-year stint in another a capella group, the Phones, Rusty started a musical comedy group called Scared Weird Little Guys with fellow member of the Phones, John Fleming. The Scaredies enjoyed an incredible 20 year career, which included an astonishing 4500 performances all over the world, playing festivals, comedy clubs, theatres, universities, countless television and radio spots, corporate events, children's shows and everything in between. After the Scaredies finished up in 2011, Rusty did the next obvious thing – he went to Antarctica and ran a marathon. He chronicled this adventure in his first book – *Scared Weird Frozen Guy: One Man's Midlife Mission from Musical Comedian to Antarctic Marathon Man*.

Also by Rusty Berther

Scared Weird Frozen Guy

WHAT, AND GIVE UP SHOWBIZ?

BEHIND-THE-SCENES TALES OF LAUGHTER AND DISASTER FROM AUSTRALIA'S TOP COMEDY ACTS

RUSTY BERTHER

Hey Stu. Thanks again + keep 'Livin' the dream!

Cheers
Rusty

The Five Mile Press

The Five Mile Press Pty Ltd
1 Centre Road, Scoresby
Victoria 3179 Australia
www.fivemile.com.au

Part of the Bonnier Publishing Group
www.bonnierpublishing.com

Copyright © Rusty Berther, 2014
All rights reserved. No part of this book may be reproduced, stored in a retrieval system, or be transmitted by any form or by any means, electronic, mechanical, photocopying, recording or otherwise, without the prior written permission of the publisher.

First published 2014

Printed in Australia at Griffin Press.
Only wood grown from sustainable regrowth forests is used in the manufacture of paper found in this book.

The stories in this book are as told to Rusty Berther. He has written them to capture the flavour of the stories and keep a consistent voice, and any direct quotes are in quotation marks.

Some of the names in this book have been changed.

National Library of Australia Cataloguing-in-Publication entry
   Berther, Rusty, author.
   What, and give up showbiz? : behind-the-scenes tales of laughter and disaster / Rusty Berther.
   ISBN: 9781743466964 (paperback)
   Theater—Australia—Anecdotes
   Actors—Australia—Anecdotes.
   Amusements—Australia.
   792.0150994

*For everyone treading the boards,
breaking a leg and living the dream*

CONTENTS

What, and give up **SHOWBIZ?** 1

That's Drano with **ONE "N"** ... 7

Didn't you used to be **SOMEBODY?** 27

Why don't you both **FUCK OFF THEN?** 47

Hello, is anybody **OUT THERE?** 71

Did he just say what I **THINK HE SAID?** 89

We don't like your kind **ROUND HERE** 109

And you **ARE ...?** 125

Yeah, nah, it was a **PRETTY BAD GIG** 157

Never work with children or **ANIMALS OR JUGGLERS** 171

I've played **EVERYWHERE, MAN** 183

They said *what* **ABOUT ME?** 197

Mum, Dad, I'm gonna **BE A COMEDIAN** 203

Two managers walk **INTO A BAR** 215

Living **THE DREAM** 217

Bad news **TRAVELS FAST** 237

Life on the **ROAD**   247

EPILOGUE   259

ACKNOWLEDGEMENTS   261

ILLUSTRATION LIST   263

What, and give up SHOWBIZ?

There is an old joke about working in the entertainment industry. You may have heard it before.

A elderly man was shovelling elephant dung at a circus when a passer-by walked up and asked, 'Is this what you do all day?'

The man stopped what he was doing, leaned on his shovel and looked at the passer-by.

'Sure is,' he said proudly, 'and I've been doing it for over 30 years.'

'Wow,' said the passer-by. 'I can't think of anything worse than shovelling elephant crap for a living. Do you ever think about quitting and getting a better job?'

The man answered, 'What, and give up showbiz?'

This joke has been told countless times and has many variations. I first heard a version based around a local rock venue, the Old Greek Theatre. Two musicians were walking through the empty auditorium after a gig when they saw an old man with a broom and a bucket head towards the front of the stage.

'What's the old dude doing?' asked one.

'Oh, that's just old George,' replied his mate. 'He's been working around here since the Seventies. He comes in here at 2 am every night after a gig and cleans up all the empty beer cans, broken glass, vomit and piss that's swimming around down in the mosh pit.

'Hey George!' he called out. 'What are you still doing here after all these years, man? Sweeping up other people's rubbish and mopping up bodily fluids isn't something that a nice old bloke like you should be doing. Isn't it time you gave up the late nights, retired and moved on to something else?'

Of course, Ol' George replied, 'What, and give up showbiz?'

It's a bit like the legendary 'Aristocrats' joke, in that it doesn't really matter how you set it up, as long as it ends with the same punchline: *What, and give up showbiz?* You could set the joke just about anywhere – a circus, a pub, a music festival, the Channel Nine boardroom – as long as the protagonist has undergone multiple years of unpleasantness while performing an undesirable task, usually involving excrement of some description.

Of course, the underlying the joke is the fact that the entertainment industry is filled with shitty jobs, and that many people will do anything to be part of the enticing world of 'showbiz'.

Including me.

I've been lucky enough to have worked in showbiz full-time since 1986. It was tough but mostly fun in the early years, and financially I scraped through with the help of the Paul Keating scholarship, or 'the dole' as it is also known. There have been good times and bad times, but in general my life hasn't mimicked the lyrics of a Led Zeppelin song, though at times I have been dazed and confused, and I once owned a black dog. Since I started out in my first 'professional' group – a barbershop quartet – I have been able to survive without ever taking on a 'real job' or resorting to crime (assuming that lying on your bio or adding stars to a review is not a crime).

I have never actually shovelled elephant dung, but I have done my fair share of metaphorical shit shovelling, just like anyone who has been in showbiz for more than a few years. I've done busking, spruiking, singing telegrams, voiceovers and emceeing; I've sung on advertising jingles, picked banjo on recording sessions, appeared in TV commercials and worked as a film extra. I've worn colourful suits, dinner suits, bathing suits, animal suits, tuxedos, dresses and everything in between. I've been Gene Simmons in a KISS cover band, dressed up as Cyndi Lauper for a video clip and can say the words 'lycra unitard' without flinching.

I've sung to toddlers, school kids, boy scouts, college students, retirees, doctors, lawyers, teachers, prisoners, accountants, psychiatrists, pharmacists, truck drivers, chiropractors, miners, football players, sailors, plumbers and Japanese tourists who thought we were the Rolling Stones.

'KISS THISS' – the KISS cover band I was in, ready to take the stage at The Old Greek Theatre, 1989. I am the baby-faced Gene Simmons on the right

(Rusty Berther)

WHAT, AND GIVE UP SHOWBIZ?

I've performed in theatres, comedy clubs, nightclubs, country pubs, theatre restaurants, state fairs, rotundas, cruise ships, barges, school halls, scout halls, concert halls, shopping malls, gala balls, churches, footy clubs, sailing clubs, courtrooms, parliaments, embassies, expos, casinos, stadiums, racetracks, sheep stations, college cafeterias, sports bars, lounge rooms, back yards, parks, hospitals, zoos, mansions, markets and mineshafts.

I've done gigs at the Sydney Opera House and the MCG, on the backs of trucks, in buses, on trains and trams, riding a bicycle, and while wearing rollerblades.

I've played weddings, funerals, birthday parties, dinner parties, sports nights, launches, Amway conventions, benefits, awards nights, trivia nights, folk festivals, street festivals, fringe festivals, fetes and fundraisers. I've played with symphony orchestras, big bands, small bands, bluegrass bands, rock bands, drummers, choirs and barbershop quartets.

I've been on talk shows, variety shows, quiz shows, kids' shows, panel shows, game shows, footy shows, current affairs shows, news broadcasts, telethons and TV galas, radio and live internet broadcasts; I've recorded one vinyl LP, nine CDs, four EPs, three cassettes and a DVD.

I've played to audiences of seven and audiences of 90,000 and travelled the world: New York, London, Hong Kong, Dubbo ...

I've been cheered, booed, applauded, heckled, ripped off, underpaid, overpaid, laughed with, laughed at, admired, despised, won awards, made friends, lost friends and come out the other side richer for the experience.

All in pursuit of living the dream.

So it would take some serious shit to happen for me to ever think of saying, 'Yes, actually I think I will give up showbiz', because usually even the bad bits are good. Especially when the bad bits can be worked up into entertaining stories you can share with your mates while hanging around backstage or in the tour van, or possibly be put into a book.

In the entertainment industry there has always been an unspoken law that 'whatever happens on the road, stays on the road' – until now.

That's Drano with ONE 'N'...

'Ladies and gentlemen, please welcome [insert correct name here]...' If only it was that simple. It doesn't matter if you're a comedian, a musician, a plumber or a teacher, unless your name is John Smith, at some point it has been misspelled or mispronounced. And even you, John Smith, may have experienced yourself being referred to as Jon Smith, Joan Smythe or Gordon Wah Wah Fnarkle, depending on the care factor of the person introducing you, which, in showbiz, is usually not very high.

Choosing a name like 'Scared Weird Little Guys' for our group seemed like a good idea at the time. When John and I first heard those four words in that order, it really stood out to us. By the way, before I go on, we got the name from a line in a movie – *Cruising*, starring Al Pacino. Al plays an undercover cop who is investigating murders in the underground gay S&M scene of New York City in the Seventies, which is obviously something that John and I could easily relate to. There is a scene where Pacino's superior, played by Paul Sorvino, says, 'There's all these scared, weird, little guys out there who don't know why they do what they do.' Once we heard that sentence, we both looked at each other and John rewound the VHS cassette and replayed it. We wrote the name down and memorised it, and it became the name of our new group; that is, once we established that 'scared, weird, little guys' wasn't code for some form of bizarre gay S&M fetish – not that there's anything wrong with that, and not that

(Rusty Berther)

there weren't other comedy duos around that had names that sounded like weird fetishes. Just don't go into an underground gay S&M club in New York and ask for a 'Lano and Woodley' is all I'm saying.

Anyway, as soon as the newly named Scared Weird Little Guys started doing gigs, we quickly realised that having a lengthy, peculiar name wasn't such a cool thing. In fact it was more frustrating and annoying than cool, because it was difficult for people to remember, or spell, or even read out off a piece of paper.

We were often introduced as the 'Sacred' Weird Little Guys, or the Sacred 'Wired' Little Guys, and plenty of times the order of the words would be mixed around, as in the Scared Little Weird Guys.

I reckon about five per cent of people in the world know how to spell the word 'weird' correctly. Along with other common 'ei' words such as 'heir', 'seize', and 'deinstitutionalising', 'weird' is one of those words that goes against the special little spelling rule

THAT'S DRANO WITH ONE "N"...

– you know, the 'i before e except after c' rhyme. Here's another spelling rhyme for you that makes it easy to remember: 'Learn the fuck how to spell the word *weird*.'

We soon learned that if someone merely got the order of the words in our name wrong, they were actually doing quite well, and that while it seemed so important to us, most people really didn't care about the name of our silly little comedy group at all. They just threw some similar-sounding words together like this:

'Hey, it's the scary funny little blokes,' or 'The silly little guys,' or 'You're one of those crazy wibbly-wobbly men, aren't you?'

Melbourne comedian Lawrence Mooney had one woman actually tape over one of the o's in his surname on a poster, as she was sure that it was a mistake and that his name was Lawrence Money, not Lawrence Mooney. Maybe she thought she *had* booked Lawrence Money, the bloke who does the gossip column in *The Age* newspaper.

Australia and Ireland's favourite Irish–Australian comedian, Jimeoin, used to go by the name Jimeoin Jimmy James when he first started doing comedy in the late 1980s, but it confused people. For simplicity he changed it back to Jimeoin, which, to this day, I am sure is spelled incorrectly. Even after two decades of success, many people think his real name is Jim Owen.

Damian Callinan, strangely, often gets introduced as David O'Callahan. Once he was talking to a booker on the phone about a gig and he was asked

Jimeoin Jimmy James' first ever publicity shot
(James Penlidis)

how to spell his name. With patience, Damian replied, 'D-A-M-I-A-N' etc., and turned up at the gig to see his name advertised as 'Roman Cowinan'.

Toronto comedian Simon Rakoff once turned up to a gig to see his name on one of those blackboards with the white letters that you change around to spell whatever it is that needs advertising. The board said, 'Comedy Show Tonight – with comedian Simon Rakotti.'

Simon found the venue manager and politely explained that his name was spelled R-a-k-o-f-f. The manager replied, 'Oh yes, I know how your name is spelled, but we needed the f's for 'Buffet'.'

A pub in Geelong that used to hold comedy nights in the late 1980s once served up a great nomination for worst attempt at getting the names of comedians correct. Glenn Robbins, Russell Gilbert and Trevor Marmalade turned up one night to see a large blackboard at the front of the venue claiming that Glenn Rubins, Russell Gilmore and Trevor Mammulate were performing that night.

Russell Gilmore and Trev Mammulate – dunno where Glenn Rubins was
(James Penlidis)

Melbourne comedy stalwart Brad Oakes would often do shows with a juggler named Pasha, and they were delighted to see themselves named in a newspaper advertisement as 'Bradley Cakes and Pasta the Juggler'.

When Lano and Woodley were first performing, it was

no surprise to hear that they had trouble with people remembering their name.

A guy who was about to introduce them asked, 'So is it pronounced Lane-o or Larn-o?'

Colin replied, 'It's Lano, as in Drano.'

Pretty straightforward, you would think, but a few minutes later the bloke got out onstage and said, 'Ladies and gentlemen, please welcome Drano and Woodley!'

Bradley Cakes and
Pasta the Juggler
(James Penlidis)

At another gig around that time, Frank and Col were introduced as 'The Empty Pockets', the name of another quite well-known comedy duo. Going on with the wrong introduction was not that bad, but when they picked up the cheque at the end of the night, it was also made out to 'The Empty Pockets'.

Even if the person introducing you gets your name correct, there's no guarantee the introduction will be all it should.

Peter Fox was brought onstage in Sydney one night with, 'Now I'm going to bring on the next act, he's not one of my personal favourites, but let's see how he goes.'

Our favourite Kiwi refugee Cal Wilson's most memorable introduction went like this: 'Ladies and gentlemen, we have two women on the bill tonight, so bear with us. Here's the first one, whose name is Cal Wilson.'

Performing with my new group, Rusty and Another Guy, I once had an emcee come over just before he was to introduce us and thrust an A4 page in front of me that was filled with paragraphs downloaded from the internet. He said roughly, 'Have a look at that and tell me if it's okay.' There was way too much information for an intro, which I think should only be a couple of sentences long, so I said, 'That's too long, mate. Just say that first line – *After 20 years of performing with the Scared Weird Little Guys, Rusty has found another guy, please welcome Rusty and Another Guy.*'

He laughed like I was joking and then proceeded to go out and read (badly) everything on the sheet, which took about five minutes and absolutely sapped the crowd. I thought, 'Why'd you even ask, you tosspot?'

Another time at the Dee Why RSL in Sydney, Marty and his dad, the legendary Maurie Fields, were doing their show called *The Father, The Son and the Holy Joke.* When they arrived at the club, they met an old friend of Maurie's named Peter Colville, who was a comedian who had come out from England with Vic Gordon in the 1950s and had performed with Maurie many times. Peter was a member of the RSL club and insisted that he should be the one to bring on Marty and Maurie.

The trouble was that Peter was now well into his eighties, and was not completely in control of all of his faculties. 'Let's just say his mind was quite addled,' was how Marty put it. So Peter went out to introduce them and started off with some rambling story about comedy in the Fifties and how he had first met Maurie, then he drifted off into some other unrelated story for a few minutes. As Peter continued on and on, Marty and Maurie, who were standing ready with their zoot suits and ukes in the wings, gradually realised that Peter had completely forgotten who he was introducing and he was trying to fill in time in the vain hope that he would remember the names of the two blokes standing waiting to go on. In the end Peter said, 'Oh well, you know who they are. Please welcome them.'

During that same tour, Marty and Maurie were completing a run of dates along the Murray River. A different local comedian had been booked to open up for each of the shows and at one of the dates the opening act sheepishly approached Marty before the show and said, 'Hey Marty, I wonder if you could help me out? I've got some good opening material, but I am really struggling to bring it home. Have you got a good closing gag that you could lend me?'

That was quite a strange thing to ask another comedian just before you are about to introduce them, but Marty said, 'Why don't you just do the mood party joke? Sure it's a bit blue, but it's a good one.'

'What's the mood party joke?' asked the young comedian.

'Well,' said Marty, 'this is how it goes. A bloke decided to throw a fancy dress party where you have to come dressed as a "mood". When it was time for the party to start there was a knock at the door and it was a guy dressed completely in green.

'"Ah," said the host, "green for envy. Well done, you can come in."

'Another knock at the door revealed a woman dressed all in blue.

'"Blue for sadness. Nice costume, please come in."

'The next bloke to arrive at the door was completely naked, with a big vat of custard around his waist on a belt, and his penis was hanging in the custard.

'"What are you?" asks the host.

'"I'm fucking dis custard," replied the man.'

The young comedian laughed and said, 'That's a good one, and it is a bit blue, though I guess I could clean it up.'

He went out onstage and when it was time to bring on Marty and Maurie he told the mood party joke. All went well until he got to the last line and said, 'So the host says to the naked man, what are you? And the man says, "I am rooting this custard".'

The scheduling of a comedy act to help lighten the announcement of bad news is a common theme that usually leads to onstage introductions that don't really set the scene for ensuing hilarity.

The Scaredies once had a difficult introduction at a college in Canada. It was a lunchtime gig and the common area was packed as the director of student activities took the stage to quieten the crowd and bring us on. He was holding a plastic bucket and said, 'Many of you know one of our popular photography students from last year named Robert Lees. We have many fond memories of his time here at the college. This year, Robert has been working as a photojournalist covering the war in Bosnia and we have just received the unfortunate news that he has been killed. We will now be passing around this bucket to take donations to help his wife and young child. On a lighter note, please welcome the Scared Weird Little Guys.'

Melbourne comedy behemoth Colin Cole was once introduced by a company CEO at a corporate dinner with the words, 'I am very sorry to announce that it has been a tough year for the company and it pains me to say that we will be cutting our total staff numbers by half. Now, please welcome some comedy by Colin Cole.'

Colin struggled through the show and after he had finished asked the CEO why he had made that announcement before bringing him on.

'I just thought it would soften the blow for them,' he explained.

Funny man Marty Fields had a similar experience while doing a gig for Ford. It was not long after they had announced they were retrenching 700 workers, many of whom were attending the gala dinner where Marty was to perform. Apparently they considered not going ahead with the dinner and then decided it was going to be cheaper to go ahead than to cancel. Unsurprisingly, the vibe in the room was a bit glum as a steady procession of senior managers spoke to everyone about why the retrenchments had to be made and where the company was headed. The last bloke to talk ended his speech by introducing Marty like this: 'We're very much aware that many of you won't be with us by the end of the year, but please put all of that to the back of your minds and try to get a laugh out of this bloke, Marty Fields.'

The Scaredies performed with Vince Sorrenti at an AFL grand final breakfast for Collingwood one year. The gig was great, possibly due to the fact that Collingwood were actually *in* the grand final that year, but more likely because the packed crowd had been sinking Crown Lagers since 8 am. As we headed off to watch the game, Vince told us he hoped that Collingwood would win because he would be back after the game performing for Collingwood's post–grand final party. It was not a good day for the Magpies, because the powerful Brisbane Lions team thrashed them by 50 points.

That night Vince was back at the same venue where we had done the breakfast, which was now only half-filled with sombre Collingwood fans. He was brought onstage with this inspiring intro: 'Well, what can I say? It's been a shit day, here's a comedian.'

Timing is everything in comedy, from an extra second's delay in the delivery of a punchline, through to the timing of material about a controversial or catastrophic event. I've spoken to many comedians and discovered that inappropriately timed introductions involving the announcement of bad news are actually quite common. But there is one story about trying to do comedy after a death announcement that tops them all …

Lano and Woodley were very excited about the debut of their long-awaited television series, *The Adventures of Lano and Woodley*. Like most television series, it had been a few years in the making, from the first meetings with UK production house Working Title, through the months spent developing the scripts, to the eventual shooting and editing that take up such a large amount of time. Negotiating a suitable on-air date and timeslot with the ABC had been filled with complications, though finally a date was selected for the show's debut: 2 September 1997. Two days after the death of Lady Diana Spencer.

Of course no one could have foreseen such an unfortunate event as the death of the People's Princess. It literally took over all television, radio and newspapers to the point that nothing else was covered, let alone two daggy dickheads and their whimsical little TV show.

For three days the ABC had shown around-the-clock coverage of the death and funeral of Lady Di, but life had to go on. They needed to resume regular programming at some point. So, with a final montage of the mangled car wreck, hysterical members of the public and wreath-laying children playing over a sad Elton John song, the coverage of one of the most reported events in history finished with these words coming up on the screen:

The ABC and all its staff offer our deepest and sincerest sympathy at the passing of the People's Princess, Lady Diana Spencer.
1/7/1961 – 31/8/1997

THAT'S DRANO WITH **ONE "N"**...

'I've got a feeling, got a bit of an inkling, this
is gonna be one of those days ...'
(James Penlidis)

The words remained on the screen for ten seconds then slowly faded away, to be replaced by the foolishly grinning face of Colin Lane, gaily singing the opening lines of *The Adventures of Lano and Woodley* theme song to a jaunty trombone and guitar riff.

Finishing off this chapter about weird introductions is a story that contains many 'What, and give up showbiz?' moments for its protagonist, Doug Chappel. The introduction Doug gets before coming onstage is my favourite part of the story, but it would equally be at home among collections of tales involving shit gigs, fights at gigs, gigs in the country, hecklers and gigs at footy clubs.

Melbourne comedian Doug Chappel had a call from his booking agent about a function for a bikie gang – yes, apparently they have functions too. He agreed because he had never done a gig like that before, plus he needed the cash. On the night of the gig, Doug turned up at the bikie compound where the gig was to be held to find two large bearded blokes standing ominously in front of the heavily fortified, windowless building.

'Can I come in?' Doug asked.

'Who the fuck are you?' demanded bearded gent #1.

'Ah, I'm the comedian for tonight,' replied Doug.

'Comedian? You better be fucken funny,' said bearded gent #2, as he unlatched the bolt on the large door and swung it open.

Message received.

The interior of the bikie clubhouse was set up like a nightclub with a bar, dance floor and a stage, upon which a blues band was playing. The president of the bikie club, who introduced himself as 'Junkyard', approached Doug, showed him around the place and told him to get to the bar and order a drink. While Doug was waiting for the bartender to mix his beer, he had a look around at the high concrete walls, barbed wire and fortified steel doors. They were either expecting some serious trouble from the cops or were hiding top Al-Qaeda leaders there.

He noted that it wouldn't be an ideal place to get into any trouble with the crowd, as there weren't exactly any beefy security guards to assist a comedian who might inadvertently offend a bikie. Security guards were unnecessary; bikies were their own security. Doug asked Junkyard if it was okay to bag someone in the crowd for a bit of fun.

'Which of these mad bastards do you want to bag?' asked Junkyard, casting his eye over the rough-looking crowd.

'No one in particular,' explained Doug, 'I just want to make sure I don't say anything to the wrong mad bastard.'

'Well, I wouldn't say anything to that bloke,' Junkyard said, pointing to a large, leather-clad chap with an eye patch.

'Nor to him, or him,' he continued, pointing around the room, 'and whatever you do, don't say anything to that group of blokes over there. See that guy at the end of the bar? He's fine. You can say anything you want to him.'

'Is there anything that I can't talk about?' asked Doug.

'Talk about whatever you want,' said Junkyard, 'just don't mention any rival bikie clubs.'

Doug told him that he had recently done some touring around the country doing shows with the infamous ex-criminal Chopper Read and that he had some funny stories about him.

'Shit, don't mention Chopper!' Junkyard exclaimed. 'That bastard once stabbed one of our members in prison.'

'Okay, so I can talk about whatever I want, except other bikie clubs and Chopper Read. Anything else you want to warn me about before I get killed?'

Doug started his gig and of course most of the crowd was shouting stuff out to him, but they were mainly up for a good time. That was, until Doug started making fun of some of their nicknames and one particular chap, called Spider, took offence and got a bit serious with Doug.

'Whaddya fucken mean by that?' Spider said aggressively. 'Are you tryin' to hang shit on me?'

'No, mate,' said Doug, who was very good at keeping rough crowds in control, 'there's only one guy I can hang shit on in here and that's the bloke over there at the end of the bar.'

They laughed at that and the rest of the gig went fine for Doug, at least fine enough that he made it out of the bikie compound alive. He received a call from his agent the next day saying that he had gone down so well the bikies wanted to book him for some of their other chapters' functions. Doug agreed, but mentioned to his agent that, while a couple of bikie gigs were fine and they were a great bunch of guys, he didn't really want to do many more and become known as the bikie comedian. During the same phone call, Doug's agent said he had a country footy club gig available in a few weeks time. It was in central Victoria and was part of a three-day fishing competition, where about 400 people camp out and fish, as well as watch a few bands.

'How long do I have to do?' asked Doug.

'Forty minutes,' replied his agent, 'and it's two sets.'

'And there'll be no bikies?' asked Doug jokingly.

'No bikies,' assured his agent.

Two 20-minute sets performing on the back of a truck to some country footy people by the banks of a river sounded rather pleasant, so he agreed to do the gig.

A few weeks later, Doug arrived in the smallish country town. He had been instructed to check in to the only motel in town. But the motel owner had no record of any booking, so Doug had to call the bloke from the footy club who had organised the gig to come and sort it out. While he was waiting, Doug noted that his was the only car in the carpark, and the motel owner confirmed that he would be the only guest that night. Everyone else was out by the river, camping on the large property that held the event.

The bloke from the footy club, whose name was Snapper, arrived. Having spent the last few days camping and setting up the site, unsurprisingly he looked dirty and had a certain fishy smell about him. He was a bit pissed off that he had had to come back into town to sort out the comedian's motel room, though he did give Doug a lift out to the site, which was about ten minutes out of town. During the silence of the car trip, his nose filled with the aroma of fish, Doug thought about the spot he was about to perform. Daytime gigs organised by a footy club would often involve families or sponsors, so Doug wanted to check if he could swear in his act.

'Can I swear during the gig?' he asked.

'What?' said Snapper.

'Is it okay to swear?' Doug asked again.

'Of course it's okay to fucken swear! Why? Don't you fucken swear?' asked Snapper.

'Well,' said Doug, 'I can swear if I want to, but –'

'Why did you fucken ask then?' snapped Snapper.

Doug could tell that there was something about him that Snapper just didn't like.

They arrived at the site and Doug noticed that, for a footy club event, there seemed to be an awful lot of motorbikes parked among the tents. As he walked through the crowd on the way to the stage he realised that about half the crowd could be described as 'living the bikie lifestyle', which is not necessarily a sign of trouble, but as Doug had found from experience, you have to watch yourself while performing to blokes with eye patches and nicknames like Spider.

'Okay, so you're doing two 40-minute spots, right?' said Snapper.

'Ah, I was told it was 40 minutes in two spots of 20,' replied Doug.

'That's bullshit,' said Snapper, 'plus we need you to host the joke competition during the break.'

Doug couldn't be bothered arguing with Snapper, who kept on having a go at him about the swearing issue, so he agreed to do the 40-minute sets, and he didn't mind hosting the joke competition because that sounded fairly straightforward. It might even be fun. They headed to the side of the stage and Doug grabbed a quick bourbon from the rider – he was going to need all the help he could get.

While Snapper climbed onto the stage to introduce him, Doug peered out and surveyed the crowd, which looked like a collection of everyone who had ever appeared on *Australia's Most Wanted*. Doug's over-waxed, styled hairdo was going to make him stand out because most of the crowd had shaved heads, goatees and neck tatts – and you should have seen what the blokes looked like ... boom tish ... Righto.

Snapper gave Doug the following introduction:

'All right you bastards, we've got the joke competition coming up and you can win 50 bucks if you can tell a good fucken joke. We got a comedian coming on first, but I want youse to get up here and show this cunt just how funny we are. Anyway, I'll bring him on. His name's Doug Chappel and apparently he "doesn't fucking swear".'

Doug walked out to the microphone and before he could say a word, a big bloke yelled out, 'Why don't you fucken swear ya poofta?' which set the tone for the start of his act. People shouted out all kinds of nasty things that made Doug instantly regret that he had agreed to do *two* 40-minute sets, let alone host the joke competition as well. He couldn't even attempt to do any material, so he ended up just insulting random members of the crowd. After about ten minutes of this, he had obviously found the level of the audience and they started warming to him, even cheering him on and eventually he felt they were getting on side. Just when he thought he could actually start doing some jokes, a massive fight broke out in the middle of the crowd. All Doug could think was that at least he could include the disruption in his 40 minutes, so he started commentating the fight.

'Ooh, there's a big left from the bloke with the eye patch. Ow! That one's gonna hurt,' etc.

When the smoke cleared from the brawl and a few large blokes had marched the offenders out, Doug finished up his first set and sat down with a few more bourbons, wondering what the hell he had got himself into. Before he had time to come to his senses and get the hell out of the place, Snapper had him back up onstage hosting the joke competition. A line of blokes formed and one by one Doug introduced a collection of the most sexist, racist and offensive jokes he had ever heard, though one of the entrants, who introduced himself simply as Boner, did tell a pretty decent joke. After a dozen contestants had been up on stage to have their turn, unsurprisingly, another fight broke out. Doug also did some blow-by-blow commentating for this second fight, which was broken up much quicker than the first one. As one of the combatants was being dragged past the stage in a headlock, he looked up with his blood-covered face and gestured at Doug, who shrugged his shoulders and said, 'What?'

'Me 50 bucks, mate! Mine was the best joke, I need me 50 bucks!' It was Boner. Someone must have taken offence at his overuse of hyperbole or something and given him an absolute pounding.

'I'll send your 50 to the hospital for you,' Doug shouted as Boner was dragged away.

With the joke competition over, Doug had a few more bourbons to fortify himself before facing the onslaught of the second set, which he completed successfully, meaning that no fights broke out. All he had to do now was find Snapper, get paid and head back to the motel, but when he asked the bar manager where Snapper was, he was informed that Snapper had gone.

'No worries, mate,' said the bar manager, 'I'll nip over and see if I can find someone to get your pay.

Doug really just wanted the whole experience to be over, and he was feeling a little pissed off while he was standing there waiting, when he saw two bikies hugging each other. That's right. Two bikies hugging each other. It had been such a long day, with the two 40-minute sets, the joke competition, the fights, the bourbons and Snapper. He couldn't help himself and humorously said something to the bikies along the lines of, 'Are you having a good time there, fellas?'

When the bikies turned around to see who had spoken, Doug thought he recognised one of them. It was Spider from the bikie gig a few weeks before.

'What the fuck do you care, you unfunny cunt?' said Spider.

'Oh, great,' thought Doug, but he wasn't afraid. Doug could handle himself okay and Spider wasn't that big, for a bikie. Plus Doug had bourbon and stage bravado on his side. He should have shut his mouth and walked away, but after receiving crap all night, he bit back with, 'Why don't you get a room then?'

A few smart comments went back and forth before the bloke arrived back with Doug's pay.

Doug grabbed it and started walking off to find his way back to the motel.

'Yeah, that's it, mate, keep walking,' shouted Spider.

Doug turned and said, 'Look, dickhead, I'm not leaving because I'm scared of you, I've just had enough of this day and I'm going.'

'You better watch your back, smartarse,' were Spider's parting words.

When Doug finally got back to the motel and had a bit of time to think about the past few hours, he realised that, Spider and his mate were probably not going to let him get away with talking to them like that. They were doubtless going to have a few more drinks and then say to themselves, 'I say, what about we go and remonstrate with that smart-mouthed chap with the stylish hairdo,' or words to that effect. Doug regretted mentioning the name of his motel during his second set, as now it would be easy for Spider to locate him. Doug's mind was racing, and he had worked himself up into a paranoid state. He couldn't just drive home, because he had drunk too much, so he looked around the motel room for ways he could prepare for Spider's arrival. First, he took the one chair in the room and wedged it against the door handle. Then he slid the bed over and wedged that against the chair, but he felt he needed more protection, so he searched around the room for a possible defensive weapon. There was the clock radio; maybe he could grip the cord and swing it aggressively like a modern day flail. His eyes fell on the neatly folded towel and little packet of soap on the bed; probably not, though that motel soap can really sting if it gets in your eyes. He was about to give up, when he spied the most deadly of all standard-issue country motel items – the butter knife.

He held it in his hand and felt the weight, then did a few practice stabs in the air. This was good, he thought, but it needed to be sharper. He wedged the knife into the doorjamb of the bathroom, leaned on it with all his weight and snapped half of the blade off to make it pointier. He then spent the next half hour scraping the blade on the floor of the concrete shower to sharpen it into a deadly weapon. A bit later, as Doug lay wide awake in his bed, wedged against the chair, wedged against the door and holding a homemade prison shank that even Chopper Read would have been proud of, he thought to himself, 'Man, I have got to get myself a new agent.'

Didn't you used to be
SOMEBODY?

'It's great, people know your name, but you don't know theirs.'
– HOMER SIMPSON, ON BEING FAMOUS.

I've never had my own show, or appeared regularly enough on television to be instantly recognisable, but I have done a couple of hundred television appearances on talk shows, variety shows, game shows, news shows, footy shows, cooking shows, the *Sale of the Century* gift shop and many other pointless shows in the pursuit of publicity, just so that a small number of people might come up to me down at the shops and go, 'Hey, Rusty!' and others will go, 'Hey, you're one of those blokes,' and many others will go, 'I think I've met you before. Where did you go to school? Do you know Steve?' Or, as someone said to me recently, 'Didn't you used to be somebody?'

I have been mistaken for the guy from Frente more times than I would have liked. I've had a guy in a video shop come up to me and thank me for putting him on to *The A-Team*.

'What are you talking about?' I said.

'I saw you on Rove, talking about *The A-Team*,' he replied.

'Ah, I believe you might be thinking of Peter Helliar,' I said.

Only a few weeks ago a guy came up to me when I was out seeing a band and said, 'Oh, excuse me mate. Wow. Listen, I just want to say that you have been a huge influence on me and because of you, I got myself a Fender Telecaster and am now playing guitar.'

'Gee,' I thought, feeling pretty good about myself, 'isn't that great, influencing a member of the public like that.' I was just about to launch into a humble, 'Well, mate, you know that anyone can achieve their dreams if they really put their mind to it,' when I thought, 'Hang on, I've never played a Fender Telecaster; in fact, I'm quite crap on the electric guitar.'

Then he said, 'Mate, when I watch you in the *RocKwiz* band, the way you play that Telecaster and then tear it up on the piano …' I should point out that I am even worse at playing the piano than I am at the Telecaster. This guy thought I was the excellent and talented James Black, leader of the *RocKwiz* band, who actually has a beard, glasses and – no offence, James – is about 15 years older than me. But I was happy to take one for team if it meant I was now the main musical muse for some bloke in a suburban pub. That didn't stop me quickly ending the conversation before he realised I was not James Black and it became awkward and embarrassing for both of us.

I was in a hot chicken shop in Ocean Grove when a bloke stopped me, looked right into my face and cheerfully said, 'Ricky!'

'No, Rusty!' I said back to him.

'Ricky Gervais!' he said.

'Mate, we're in a hot chicken shop in Ocean Grove,' I replied. 'I'm not Ricky Gervais …'

A friend was once talking to her mum, who said, 'I heard Rusty on the radio the other day.'

'That's nice,' said my friend.

'Yes,' said her mum, 'except there's three of them now, and they're called Tripod.'

Of course, it works both ways, as Scod from Tripod found out when he was travelling through Adelaide airport one day and was approached by a bloke who pointed at him and said, 'Hey, Scared Weird Little Guys!'

DIDN'T YOU USED TO BE **SOMEBODY?**

Tripod in their younger days – that's Moby on the left
(James Penlidis)

Scod said, 'Ah no, Tripod actually.'

The bloke said, 'Same diff' and walked away.

Colin Lane had an experience with someone coming up to him in the street and saying, 'Hey! You're that guy from the Umbilical Brothers!'

'Ah, no, I am actually Colin from Lano and Woodley,' he replied.

'No,' said the bloke, 'You *are* that guy from the Umbilical Brothers.'

'No, mate, I'm telling you, I know who I am, and I'm not the guy from the Umbilical Brothers,' said Colin, a little more forcefully this time.

'Oh,' said the stranger, 'That's okay then, because I don't really like the Umbilical Brothers anyway,' and walked off.

Yon, the diminutive, angel-voiced Tripod chap with the prominent skull, had a member of the public approach him, point and say, 'Moby Dick!'

'What?' replied Yon.

'Moby Dick,' the man repeated, pointing at him again.

The penny dropped for Yon, who said, 'Oh, yeah, some people tell me I look like that DJ – Moby.'

'Yeah, Moby Dick!' said the guy again, as Yon started to think that those were the only words the man could say.

Sometimes I will get this 'Excuse me, I love your work and there's this friend of ours who looks exactly like you and do you think we could get a photo with both of you, please?'

So I'll walk over to their little group and they stand me next to some stunted, rotund, grotesque-looking troll of a man for a photo and I think, 'Dear God, is this really how I appear to people?'

Being mistaken for other acts is one thing, but it is an interesting realisation that being part of a group where you spend an inordinate amount of time thinking about your act, the direction you want to head in, your public profile and how the general public perceive you, to know that you essentially don't mean very much to most people. Having not pursued that course for a few years now, it is actually quite refreshing to realise that 99 per cent of people don't really care what the real name of your act is or what you are trying to create artistically, you are just, 'some bloke off the telly'.

Corinne Grant was in the middle of a country tour and was travelling by herself. She had checked into a motel in Foster, in country New South Wales.

'I see you're travelling by yourself, will you be joining us in the restaurant for dinner?' asked the proprietor, in that friendly way of country motel owners who consider your personal business their personal business.

'Oh, I guess so,' replied Corinne.

'Good, we'll seat you with another female traveller who is also by herself, so you can have a bit of company while you're eating your dinner.'

Corinne thought that the owner was either very friendly, or was possibly trying to start up a lesbian dating service.

Over a chicken Kiev, Corinne met the other solo traveller and she was interested to learn that her dining companion travelled all over the country selling greeting cards. That is a job that I thought became redundant in about 1972, or possibly this woman was like one of those guys in the jungle who think that the Vietnam War never ended, and she has just been driving around Australia in an HQ Holden selling her ever-so-slowly dwindling stock of greeting cards.

'Greeting cards – that's fascinating! Oh, I should introduce myself – Nicole Burchmore, pleased to meet you'
(James Penlidis)

After dinner an older couple who had been dining not far from Corinne and her new friend came over and said, 'Oh, excuse me and sorry to bother you, but my husband and I are having an argument about who you are. My husband thinks that you're Nicole Kidman, but I think that you're Rhonda Burchmore.'

When *The Panel* was still on television, Corinne was approached by a man in the street one day who said, 'I saw you breast-feeding on *The Panel*.'

'Nope, that wasn't me,' said Corinne.

'Yes you were, you were on there breast-feeding your baby.'

He was quite insistent until Corinne said, 'Look, I am pretty sure I would have remembered doing that. I probably would have also remembered giving birth. You're thinking of Kate Langbroek.'

You would think that with over 20 years of regular television exposure on some of Australia's most popular shows such as *The Comedy Company, Fast Forward* and *Kath and Kim,* Glenn Robbins would have no problems with being mistaken for somebody else. He often gets asked, 'Where did you go to school?' by some squinty-eyed member of the public with a gaping mouth.

'Strathmore High,' Glenn replies, to which squinty-eye will respond, 'No, you didn't!'

Glenn also had this exchange with a man working in a delicatessen:

'Hey, mate, I know you! You're Colin Carpenter aren't you? From that show – that comedy show?'

Colin Carpenter was a character on *The Comedy Company* that was played by the actor Kim Gyngell.

'No,' said Glenn, shaking his head, 'I am definitely not Colin Carpenter.'

The bloke behind the counter paused for a second and then said knowingly, 'Ahh, I see what you're doing. You don't want anyone to know, do you?' He winked at Glenn and whispered, 'It's okay, Colin, your secret's safe with me.'

Footy Show joke man Trevor Marmalade was on holiday in Queensland with his wife and kids when they decided to visit

Steve Irwin's Australia Zoo. They rocked up and paid the regular entry fee, and just as they got through the gate a woman came rushing out of the office saying, 'Oh, I can't believe it's you! We are so happy you chose to visit us here. Would you like to have a VIP behind-the-scenes tour for you and your family?'

'Sure thing,' said Trev, feeling a bit chuffed. He had met Steve on a couple of occasions, so he wasn't completely surprised by the offer.

They were then taken around the park on a private tour, hand-feeding birds and crocodiles, nursing koalas and petting any fluffy, furry or feathery beast that was placed in front of them. After a few pampered hours they were personally escorted back to their car by the woman who had first approached them, who said, 'Thanks again for visiting, we hope you had a wonderful day, Mr Guest.'

Mr Guest? As in Rob Guest, the musical theatre star who, it must be said, does bear quite a resemblance to Trevor Marmalade.

What could Trev say to that, apart from, 'Okay then, thanks for having us'? I would have liked it if the woman had said, 'One more thing, Mr Guest, before you go could you sing us a bit of something from *Phantom of the Opera*? Please, Mr Guest?'

The always delightful and hilarious Denise Scott had not long made the jump from stand-up comedy and perennial panel show guest to mainstream Aussie television drama as part of the cast of the successful show *Winners and Losers* when she was bailed up in the toilets of a large theatre by a woman who said, 'Oh wow! You look just like that woman from that show *Winners and Losers*! That's amazing! I can't believe how much you look like her!'

Denise smiled and said, 'Well, that's because I am her.'

'Oh my God!' said the woman. 'You sound just like her as well!'

Russell Gilbert, for some reason, often gets mistaken for Dave Hughes, which he doesn't mind because he reckons Hughesy is very funny. What Russell didn't find funny was the time he was approached by a bloke in the street who thought he was Trevor Marmalade. That was fine, as Russell thinks that Trev is a funny bastard too, but before he could correct the bloke he said to Russell, 'Yeah, you're much funnier than that Russell Gilbert, I don't find him funny at all.'

By the way, Dave Hughes was once asked after a gig, 'So, how did you come up with the name?'

You don't need to be a performer to be mistaken for someone famous. An old mate of mine, Steve, was at the races one day, making his way through the crowd when a woman stopped him and said, 'Oh my God! You're the lead singer of the Hoodoo Gurus!' Now Steve does bear a passing resemblance to Dave Faulkner, though Steve neither confirmed nor denied the accusation, as the woman was very pretty and led him over to meet all her cute friends, who proceeded to buy him a few drinks and for the next hour Steve played his role perfectly harmlessly until he thought he should get back to his mates and say his goodbyes to the women.

'Oh, we have to get your autograph!' they cried, handing him a pen and paper.

'Sure thing,' said Steve, thinking, 'If only I could remember what the hell is the name of the lead singer of the Hoodoo Gurus.'

He made a big deal out of spelling all of their names correctly, inscribed a lavish signature with plenty of loops and possibly a crossed 't' and faded off into the crowd, never to be seen again.

Lawrence Mooney was in a taxi in Sydney with fellow comedian Lehmo. The Vietnamese driver had been chatting with them both during the short trip and when they reached their destination the driver said to Lawrence, 'Tank you Mista Donut.'

Lawrence said, 'What?'

'Donut! You look like donut!' said the driver.

'A donut? You think I look like a donut?!' exclaimed Lawrence.

'No!' said the taxi driver, laughing. 'Donut! Mista Donut! You know John Howard's friend, with the curly hair. You look like Mista Donut!'

Lehmo finally got it. 'Oh, *Downer*! He means you look like Alexander Downer!'

'Yeah, dat's it, you look like Mista Alexander Downer!' said the taxi driver again.

Lehmo was lying down in the back seat of the taxi, laughing so hard he couldn't move.

Brad Oakes was in the Revolver nightclub after a long night out. It was the wrong side of 5 am when a bloke walked up to him, handed him a Black Russian and said, 'That's for you, mate.'

'What for?' asked Brad.

'That's for what you did for my sister,' the bloke replied.

'What did I do for your sister?' said Brad.

'You got my sister off heroin,' he said.

Brad replied, 'Mate, I think I've turned more people onto drugs than off them.'

'You're Les Twentyman, aren't you?' said the bloke.

'I am not Les Twentyman,' said Brad, who over the next five minutes had to eventually bring out his driver's licence to prove to the bloke that he wasn't Les Twentyman. In the end the bloke finally accepted that Brad was not Les Twentyman and said, 'Oh well, do you still want that Black Russian?'

Glenn Robbins was boarding a plane early one morning and standing in line in the aisle, waiting to take his seat, when he was recognised by someone who was already seated. You know the situation – you're sitting in your seat with nothing better to do than check out all the people walking down the aisle to their seats, when you spot someone who looks a bit familiar, though you can't quite place them. Your mind is a bit foggy because you've woken up at 5 am, fought traffic and airport security, paid $23 for a lukewarm coffee and a stale muffin, then rushed to make your 7 am flight. You sit near the entrance to the departure gate because you want to board the plane early and because you are a tool. When you finally take your seat, you see someone you know walking onto the flight so you think you'd better say hello, but you just can't nail exactly who the person is. Your mind starts going through the options: 'Did I go to school with that person? Yes! It's Johnno from Dimboola High! No, it isn't.' You think, 'Johnno had acne. Is it one of the guys from the indoor cricket club you played with after uni? No, they weren't that tall. Maybe he used to drink at the Baker's Arms when you were going out with that girl who worked at Dracula's in '95? No …

maybe he's from the telly, ah yes, that's it! Was he on *Rove*? No ... I've got it!'

'Glen!' you call out, as Glenn Robbins looks at you like someone who has had their name called out by a complete stranger.

'Glen Ridge! *Sale of the Century*!' you blurt into the awkward silence which dominates the boarding process of early morning flights, somehow thinking that a famous person should be amazed and delighted by you suddenly stating their name.

Glenn just nodded uncomfortably, lips pursed, and wished the buffoon in the sweaty tracksuit three people ahead of him in the line would hurry the fuck up and get his ridiculously oversized carry-on bag stowed so Glenn could take his seat in relative anonymity. A few minutes later he settled into his seat, happy to see that the man next to him was not gawking curiously at him, trying to work out just where the hell he knew him from.

Half an hour later, the flight had levelled out at 239,000 feet or whatever it was, and Glenn and his neighbour were watching the tiny communal television screen that folded down from underneath the overhead baggage compartment. On came an episode of *Kath and Kim* and Glenn thought, 'Oh, well, this is a bit embarrassing, isn't it. Now this bloke is going to recognise me and it's going to get a bit awkward.'

But the bloke couldn't have cared less about who was sitting next to him. He was smiling and laughing at all the appropriate places when Glenn was on the screen, but he was completely oblivious to the fact that the actor was seated next to him. He even laughed so hard at one point that he turned and looked at Glenn while pointing at the screen to share the funny moment, but then just turned back to continue his enjoyment of *Kath and Kim* without knowing he was sitting next to Glenn Robbins, or even Glen Ridge from *Sale of the Century*.

Brian Nankervis, co-creator and adjudicator of *RocKwiz*, first came to the attention of many people while performing as the eccentric beat poet character Raymond J. Bartholomew on *Hey Hey It's Saturday*. He is still sometimes recognised from those days, as in, 'Hey, you're Raymond J. Bartholomew!' or sometimes, 'Hey, you're that poetry poof from *Hey Hey*!'

One week on the *Hey Hey* talent segment called 'Red Faces', a five-year-old Raymond J impersonator named Matt came on to do a spot. He was such a huge hit that he was invited back on the show twice more to perform with Raymond J. They even did a show together at the Adelaide Fringe Festival that year and recorded a single.

Still today, when Brian gets recognised as 'that poet bloke from *Hey Hey*', people will often ask, 'Hey, where's the kid? Do you still work together?' That's an interesting thing about television. To some people, the kid hasn't grown up, despite Brian not having seen Matt for the past 18 years, and Matt now being about 23 years old.

Dave O'Neil was once standing on the footpath outside a house he was holidaying in up at Byron Bay. A man with long dreadlocks rode past on a bicycle and yelled out, 'Hey, it's Mikey Robbins! How're you going, funny man?' Then he rode off down the street laughing to himself. Dave's wife said to him, 'Why didn't you correct him and tell him that you're not Mikey?'

Dave replied, 'Oh, he was on a bike and it doesn't matter, it's not like I'll ever see him again. Let the guy think that he just saw Mikey Robbins.'

The next day at about the same time, Dave was standing out the front of the house again when a minibus full of backpackers drove past, driven by the same dreadlocked man, who got on a microphone and said, 'Hey, look everyone, it's funny man Mikey Robbins!' The following day, Dave walked into the local pub for a meal and before long heard the now familiar strain of dreadlocked man's voice saying' 'Hey, everyone, it's funny man Mikey Robbins.'

'That's not Mikey Robbins, you idiot,' Dave heard one of the dreadlocked man's friends say. 'That's Dave Hughes!'

Radio and television host Lehmo has an ongoing problem being mistaken for the same person.

He was attending the launch of a new television series and a bloke came over and interrupted his conversation with the common and well-meaning interjection, 'Oh, excuse me, mate, sorry but I just wanted to say I'm a big fan and I loved that article you wrote in *GQ* magazine – very funny.'

Lehmo's first reaction was to give the guy the benefit of the doubt, smile and nod and say sincerely, 'Thanks, mate,' even though Lehmo knew he had not written any articles for *GQ* magazine. Then the bloke went on, 'I love your radio show and I was listening to it in Sydney yesterday afternoon.'

Now Lehmo knew he was being mistaken for someone else – the giveaway being that Lehmo's radio show is in Melbourne, and is on in the morning. The bloke thought that Lehmo was Wippa from the Fitzy and Wippa radio show in Sydney, and the same thing has happened to him a dozen other times, including live on television during the show *Before the Game*, when a current AFL coach told Lehmo he listened to him all the time, despite him living in a different city. Lehmo is a difficult name to get right. It's easy to say, until you have to write it down, but at least he doesn't get introduced with 'Please welcome, Lamo' as much as he used to. After being introduced as 'Lehmo, the comedian', Lehmo has also had: 'Oh yes, I've heard of you. You're from Lehmo and Woodley.'

It always seems to be the case that when these mistaken identity incidents occur, it is usually with someone:

A. More famous than you are.

B. Someone who is doing more exciting and higher profile work than you are, and

C. You consider them to be less talented than yourself.

Okay, the third answer is not really relevant, because I am yet to meet anyone in this industry who doesn't consider everyone else to be less talented than themselves.

Cases of mistaken identity in showbiz are not restricted to just looking like another performer. A woman came up to the Scaredies after a show in Orange in New South Wales. During the show she had been shouting out for us to sing the 'Only Gay Eskimo' song, which is not our song. It is a very funny song written and performed by the Canadian group Corky and the Juice Pigs. So this woman kept on saying in a whining kind of really Aussie accent 'Aww, youse didn't play the gay Eskimo song,' and I kept saying 'That's because it's not our song.' But this woman refused to believe me and kept saying things like, 'But it *is* your song! I seen it on the telly!' Then I would say something like 'No, it's *not* our song, that's why we didn't do it tonight.' This tedious exchange went on for what seemed like half an hour until finally I said firmly, 'Look, it's not our song. It's a song by Corky and the Juice Pigs, and there's three of them.'

That was it for her. She lowered her voice and spoke slowly, clearly and quite aggressively and said, 'It *is* your song and there was *two* of youse, not three.'

Everything went quiet. I looked at John and he looked at me. Nobody said anything for about five seconds then I said, 'You're right. Of course it's our song and of course there's only two of us. Have a great night and be sure to come back and see us next time we are in Orange.' Sometimes people just don't hear what they don't want to hear.

When I told the Tripod boys that story, they laughed, as they swear they have had an almost identical conversation about the same song – possibly with the same woman. Tripod are also beginning to get a similar question about a song known as the 'Four Chords Song' by the new Sydney act, Axis of Awesome.

Lano and Woodley used to do a song called 'Sonya'. It was a cute little ditty with a catchy chorus that went,

I picked onya, I picked onya, Sonya.
I picked onya Sonya, 'cos I had a crush onya.

The number of times the Scaredies were asked to play that bloody song was ridiculous. After a while we would just roll our eyes and sing it, just the same as Lano and Woodley.

A woman once said after a show, 'Your version of "Sonya" sounded different tonight.'

'Yes,' I said, 'because you just heard it sung in tune, daahling …'

Only kidding, of course. Lano and Woodley are both fine musicians. Frank is an accomplished guitarist and Col has a lovely singing voice and often sings in tune.

That song 'Sonya' once made us a hundred bucks. The Scaredies were playing a tour of Queensland with Steady Eddy and Bruno Lucia. It was February and hot as hell but those guys

WHAT, AND GIVE UP SHOWBIZ?

Bruno Lucia as his alter ego 'Dino Valentino' –
Hey Dino, play that Sonya song
(James Penlidis)

were good company and we had a great time playing a variety of weird gigs in pubs, football clubs and RSLs up and down the Queensland coast.

The show was performed in two halves. Bruno opened up and brought Steady Eddy on to finish the first half. There was an interval, then Bruno came out again and brought us on to close the show. In a bizarre programming decision, there was an afternoon gig booked at the Redcliffe Dolphins Leagues Club, and even before the show started it felt a little strange to be doing a performance at that time of the day. It certainly got more strange as the afternoon progressed.

We were on in the 'Dolphins Showroom', which could have also been called the 'Dolphins Rectangular Room with a Glass Wall with a View of the Pokies Area Showroom'. John and I were hanging around the backstage area, which was actually just the empty kitchen. The lunch service had finished, so it doubled as the dressing room for the entertainers. It wasn't so bad, but there was a lingering aroma of chicken nuggets and something that smelled like gravy. We were standing around talking and playing a game called 'How much salmonella is in this cooking implement?' when we noticed a bloke had wandered, or should I say staggered, in from the adjacent pokies area. He looked just as surprised to see us as we were to see him. In appearance he was a little rough around the edges, shall we say, though the gaps in his teeth were perfectly balanced by the tattoos on his neck. He held a rum and Coke in each hand, and he froze as he saw us, which provided an unusual scene. He had a crazed look in his eye and as he stood there unmoving, leaning slightly forward with his feet apart, he had the stance of a Wild West outlaw ready for a gunfight, except he was holding rum and Cokes instead of six-shooters.

We looked at each other without saying anything for a while, then he gestured towards us with one of the rum and Cokes and loudly said, 'Oh, you're those fucken guys, aren't youse!'

We didn't say anything.

'Youse are those fucken guys that sing that fucken song! What the fuck's it called? Fucken Sonya that's it! I fucken love that fucken song. Are youse gonna fucken sing that fucken Sonya song now?'

Believe me, it was neither the time nor the place to be saying that it wasn't our song and that we weren't going to be singing the fucken Sonya song.

I think he could tell by the stunned looks on our faces that we needed a little extra persuasion, so he carefully, and with extreme focus, put his drinks down on a bench and reached behind his back to pull out of his jeans what I thought was going to be a knife but was actually a roll of $50 bills. He peeled off two and threw them towards us saying, 'There ya fucken go! I'll give youse a hundred bucks if youse sing that fucken Sonya song.'

'Um, we're about to go onstage, so we'll see what we can do,' I ventured.

That seemed to satisfy him so he turned his attention away from us and on to trying to pick up his two rum and Cokes with one hand. It was like watching a monkey with a puzzle. He couldn't seem to work out how on earth he had been holding both rum and Cokes only a few seconds ago yet now they just didn't seem to fit. He was slightly startled when he noticed that he did indeed have another (empty) hand attached to his other arm. A dim light bulb clicked somewhere in his head, some gears clanked and he picked up his other drink and wandered back out of the door.

John and I discussed our options.

'Right,' I said, picking up the two $50 notes and putting them in my pocket. 'I believe we have three options here. We could do the song and keep the hundred bucks, or we could *not* do the song, then find the bloke after the show, say sorry, and give him his hundred bucks back, or we could be really nice guys, do the song *and* give him his hundred back.'

After a ridiculous amount of discussion, most of which was based around our fear of being stabbed, we decided on the third option, as it left virtually no room for upsetting the Sonya man. Even if he realised that we weren't Lano and Woodley or, 'those fucken guys that sing that fucken Sonya song' or whatever he thought our name was, he would get his hundred bucks back and we would happily leave the venue without any permanent scarring.

We went onstage and started our set, though I couldn't stop thinking about the Sonya man and wondering if we had made the correct decision. He had given us the hundred bucks after all, so it

DIDN'T YOU USED TO BE **SOMEBODY?**

So then he said, 'Are youse gonna sing that fucken Sonya song?'
and I said, 'Give us a hundred bucks and we'll do it!'
(Peter Milne)

wouldn't matter if we just did the Sonya song and got it out of the way. Also, judging by his obvious inebriation, it was highly likely that he could simply forget all about our verbal contract and would be none the wiser no matter what we did. We were about three songs into our set when I noticed a commotion in the pokies area through the glass wall at the side of the room. Two burly bouncers were forcefully escorting the Sonya man through the room and out of the doors of the venue. His shirt had lost a few buttons and his treasured rum and Cokes were nowhere to be seen.

It took a few moments to sink in, but eventually I realised that Sonya man had solved our Sonya problem all by himself, and we could continue the show without doing the Sonya song and we got to keep the hundred bucks. My mind flicked through the possibilities and it looked like it was all going to be fine, unless Sonya man was waiting for us after the gig.

At the completion of the show, we came offstage and thankfully couldn't see Sonya man anywhere. We certainly wasted no time in packing up our gear and getting out to the van, and were sitting there counting our blessings, and our $50 bills, when Steady Eddy shouted from the front seat, 'Shit, there he is!' John and I hit the floor in panic to the sound of the side-splitting laughter of the rest of the van cracking up at Eddy's 'joke'. Sonya man was nowhere to be seen.

So thanks for that hundred bucks, Sonya man, whoever and wherever you are. Of course John and I thought that the fair thing to do would be to split the money with Frank and Col the next time we saw them, unless we forgot about it before we saw them. Now, where was I?

Why don't you both FUCK OFF THEN?

It is generally understood that when some drunken fool in the audience heckles a comedian they must respond immediately or lose face. Ask any working comedian who has been around for a while, and they will tell you that heckling has changed since the Eighties, when there was a tendency to actually engage with the comedian onstage, sometimes even to the benefit of the show. Back then comedians needed to be armed with an arsenal of witty put-down lines, and there was an unwritten rule that you could even use another comic's put-down if it was on the spur of the moment and you were in the frontline of a heckler-versus-comedian battle. Lines like these:

'Yes, I remember my first beer.'

'Sorry, I don't speak alcohol.'

'I can't believe it. One hundred million sperm and you were the one that got through!'

'There's an alcoholic who doesn't want to remain anonymous.'

'I'm not really good with hecklers, but a friend who is good with them wrote something down for me.' The comedian takes a piece of paper from his pocket and pretends to read from it before saying, 'Oh, yeah. Fuck off!'

These days at a comedy venue, interruptions are more likely to be people simply talking and/or ignoring the act that is onstage, or a drunk buffoon shouting out something inaudible. A newer problem is the use of mobile phones during the performance – not talking, but texting, which is just as much of a distraction to the person onstage as it is to the surrounding audience members.

When people use their phones to text or type important social media status updates, they don't realise that they are fully visible from the stage, as the phone lights up their face. The colour of the light tells the comedian what they are doing on the phone. As Brad Oakes says: 'If I can see the person's chin lit with white light, they're on Facebook, if it's blue, they're on Twitter.'

He bailed up a woman in the front row at a show once and said to her, 'Would you mind not texting on your phone during my show?'

She replied, 'I'm just texting my friend.'

Brad said, 'And what is so important that it can't wait until the end of the show?'

'If you really want to know, I'm telling my friend how funny you are,' she said smugly.

'Well, I am only halfway through the show,' said Brad.

Jack Dee, a UK comedian and regular visitor to Australia, had an excellent comeback line. After staring in the direction of the heckler, he would say in a deadpan voice to the rest of the crowd, 'Well, it's a night out for him, isn't it?' After the laughter had subsided he would add, 'For his family, it's a night off.'

A comedian friend once scored a gig as an emcee at a strip club. The kind of gig where you really don't want to go on for too long as, to put it mildly, the audience is not really there for the comedy. He introduced the first 'dancer' and after her spot was over he walked back onstage, told his first joke and someone yelled out, 'Bring back the real cunt!'

American comedian Allan Havey tells how one night he was paying out on a guy in the front row who had been talking. After silently enduring Allan's torrent of abuse for a few minutes, the guy simply looked straight up at Allan and slowly opened his suit jacket to reveal a pistol in a holster. Without skipping a beat, Allan quickly changed the subject and continued on with show.

UK comedian and regular visitor to Australia Dave Gorman was introduced one night with this: 'I've never seen this guy before. He might be good, he might be shit. I think he's a poet.' Dave walked on to the sound of 150 people chanting, 'Fuck off!' He obviously wasn't walking onstage in a funny enough manner for that audience. He then just argued with hecklers for 20 minutes and at one point he looked over and even the bar staff were heckling him.

There was a notorious gig at the Royal Hotel in Ryde involving some very organised heckling. The hotel held a weekly comedy night, attended by a diverse crowd. There were locals and bikies and students – a real mix. There was one group of local blokes who used to go every week and after a while they got to pretty much know everyone's routines. They would gather before the gig each week and see who was on, and then prepare heckle lines for specific bits of each comedian's material. They were actually a great bunch of guys and they got very creative with their heckles, but it was tough if they were targeting you.

After a while comedians wouldn't work there, so it was kind of a self-defeating practice.

Tommy Dean was in the middle of a tough gig one night at the Comedy Store in Sydney when a woman called out something during a pause in his routine. Tommy is not from the 'pay out on the heckler' school, and usually just confidently goes with the flow and jokes around with anything that gets called out. But this particular night he was already feeling a little testy and for some reason the heckle just sent him over the edge. Even though he hadn't heard exactly what was said, he launched a tirade of abuse at the poor woman, utilising all his expansive vocabulary to really give her a thorough dressing down. When he had finished, the crowd was a silent and a bit stunned and he heard the woman's voice say quietly, 'All I said was that I liked your shirt ...'

UK comedian Steve Bowditch used to head out onstage with a large, inflatable strawberry hanging off the end of his guitar. One night he walked on and a heckler yelled out, 'What are you doing with that stupid prop?'

Steve replied, 'Oh, come on mate, it's just there for a bit of fun.'

The heckler said, 'I was talking to the strawberry ...'

There is a story regarding heckling that has done the rounds of the comedy circuit for many years, and it deserves to be told here. It involves a fellow named Joel Douglas, who happens to be the younger brother of actor Michael Douglas and the son of Kirk Douglas.

Joel is a movie producer who likes to try a bit of stand-up comedy in his spare time. During a gig in the UK, Joel found himself the victim of incessant heckling, which was getting the best of him.

'Don't you know who I am?' he said, getting frustrated. 'I'm Kirk Douglas's son!'

An audience member promptly stood up and said, in reference

to Kirk Douglas's famous scene in the movie *Spartacus*, 'No, *I* am Kirk Douglas's son!' On the other side of the room, another person stood and repeated, 'No, *I* am Kirk Douglas's son!' followed by another dozen audience members.

American stand-up Adam Newman was headlining at a club in Atlanta, where a particularly annoying heckler had been bothering all of the comedians who had been on. When Adam came out onstage, the heckler's seat was empty, but his jacket was still hanging over the back of his chair. Adam was chatting to the crowd about the guy, asking where he had gone and was he coming back, and then decided that it would be a bit of fun to put on his jacket and be wearing it when the bloke took his seat again. The heckler's wife actually passed the jacket up to Adam on the stage and he promptly started riffling through the pockets after a bit of encouragement from the crowd. He found some coins, a receipt and a small plastic bag with a white powder in it. Adam quickly returned the bag to the pocket and handed the jacket back.

Once the heckler returned to his seat he remained there for the rest of the show, and Adam noted that he seemed a very awake and alert member of the audience.

Canadian comedian Guy Earle was ordered to pay a heckler CA$15,000 (AUD$15,768) in 2011, after the British Columbia Human Rights Tribunal found that he was guilty of 'causing injury to dignity, feelings and self respect'.

In 2007 Mr Earle was hosting an open mic night at a Vancouver restaurant. When the female heckler, who was a lesbian, kissed her partner and booed one of his jokes, he unleashed a profanity-laden rant, where he repeatedly attacked the woman's sexuality. She verbally abused him back and there was a minor altercation where she threw water on him and he broke her sunglasses. To cut a long story short, she lodged a case with the British Columbia Human Rights Tribunal, seeking damages for 'lasting physical and psychological effect'. The case and subsequent appeals were held over the following six years, with the tribunal eventually upholding the decision in favour of the heckler. The case inspired masses of public and online debate about free speech, discrimination, litigation and heckling.

Of course, she could have simply walked out of the club before the altercation escalated, and he could have not said things like, 'You're not even real lesbians; no guy will fuck you, that's why you're with each other.'

Judith Lucy once received a marriage proposal from a man in the audience that went, 'Will you marry me, Judith Lucy?' Judith remembers thinking at the time, 'I don't think that the surname is entirely necessary in that question, unless of course Judith Durham is standing just around the corner and the guy was tossing up between the two of us.'

On Wil Anderson's first trip to Edinburgh he was doing a show with an audience of about 12 people – which is quite good for an Edinburgh crowd. During the show he had an enthusiastic heckler with a thick Glaswegian accent shouting out constantly. Apart from disrupting the show, Wil couldn't understand a word the guy was saying. Everyone else in the crowd was more interested in listening to the heckler than the show, so Wil stopped and said, 'Mate, what is it you're trying to say?'

The heckler said in his thick Scottish brogue, 'Australians are so lazy, they wouldn't pull a greasy stick out of a dog's arse!'

This statement cracked up the rest of the audience, who

laughed like they were at a Billy Connolly show.

Wil thought he should just ignore the comment and get on with it, then he realised that this bloke wasn't just insulting him – he was insulting the whole of Australia, so he felt a patriotic pang of responsibility to respond to the bloke.

Wil shrugged his shoulders and said, 'Mate, as a proud Australian, I don't reckon we give a shit. In fact I reckon we're a little more concerned about why Scottish people are sticking the greasy stick up there in the first place. I mean, how bad are you guys at playing fetch? What happens when you pull it out anyway? Do you hold it up and say "Och, I'm king of all England"?'

Wil Anderson
(James Penlidis)

Malcolm Hardee's infamous comedy club the Tunnel in south-east London gained a reputation as a tough place to play that surpassed even Late and Live at the Gilded Balloon in Edinburgh.

The Tunnel was started in 1984 and it quickly became a legendary place to perform. Simon Munnery, a comedian who did many gigs there, described it as being by far the toughest club he has ever experienced.

He said, 'The crowd used to boo the acts on, and then "coin" them off by throwing coins at them. You couldn't really even do any material there and it helped if you treated the whole thing like a bit of a game, then the crowd would be a bit more tolerant because it was like a game to them.'

He was introduced one time to the standard chorus of boos but he merely stood at the microphone smiling and when the booing stopped, calmly said in a charming voice, 'Good evening,' to which there was a great cheer. He tried one joke and the chorus of booing returned, as well as chants of 'Off! Off! Off!', along with a rain of coins. As he exited the stage, the booing and jeering immediately turned to shouts of, 'More! More!' so he returned to the microphone as the shouts again turned into boos, said, 'Good evening,' and repeated the whole sequence another three times.

When Malcolm Hardee was compering, he would sometimes introduce inexperienced comedians with the line, 'This next act's probably a bit shit,' but he would also be completely encouraging to any of the new acts that showed potential.

Accomplished comedians, as well as beginners, found it difficult to perform there and it was generally accepted that you would either die and get booed off, or completely storm it if you managed to be accepted by the merciless crowd.

Another time, an open-mic comedian was 'hummed' off by the crowd – an example of unspoken group intelligence that would fascinate an animal behaviourist.

Simon Munnery says he has never experienced such high-calibre heckling as he received at the Tunnel, and was once abused in Latin.

Jim Tavare responded to a taunt of 'Fuck off!' with the reply, 'I'm warning you, mate, I'll have you know I'm a schizophrenic,' to which the reply came, 'Well why don't you both fuck off then!'

WHY DON'T YOU BOTH FUCK OFF THEN?

In 1984, long before they were all household names in Australia, Peter Rowsthorn, Glenn Robbins and Maryanne Fahey were doing a show at Melbourne's legendary venue the Last Laugh. At one point they called for everyone to put their hands in the air and clap. One woman wasn't participating and was singled out by Maryanne until the woman held up her arms to reveal that she wasn't raising her hands because she didn't have any. Okay ...

In the late 1980s, Tim Smith was doing a gig at the Barwon Club Hotel in Geelong with fellow comedians Russell Gilbert and Mark Neal. It was a Friday night and they had all driven down to Geelong in Mark's car for the once-a-month comedy night organised by a local promoter called Gordon. Russell was to close the night, Tim was doing first spot and Mark was the compere. The middle section of the show was dedicated to an ingenious segment called 'drink for a joke', where audience members could get up onstage and tell a joke. If the joke was deemed to be funny, they would get a free drink. This spot was intended to provide a bit more entertainment for the crowd and also ensured that the promoter didn't have to pay another comedian.

Mark Neal started up the show and the crowd was in a rowdy mood. That day, two merchant navy vessels had parked or de-shipped, or whatever it is ships do when they come into port, right there in Geelong harbour. So there were a few tables of thirsty sailors out looking for some comedy after a few months at sea.

One of the sailors at the front table had a mean-looking crew-cut and was being particularly loud. He was participating in a spirited heckling duel with Mark Neal. Like I said, in those days, shouting out mindless insults at comedians was a popular pastime amongst the fuckwit community and Mark Neal was bringing out all the big guns:

'Listen, I like doing my act the way you like having sex – alone.'

'Ladies and gentlemen, this is what happens when cousins fuck.'

Mark was hammering this guy with all these lines and the guy continued to say things like, 'Fucking tell a joke you cockhead!' and Mark said, 'I'd like to tell a joke, but every time I try there's a big fat fuckwit in the audience that keeps shouting shit out.' So they're going back and forth at each other and about half the crowd was getting a few laughs out of it, but crew-cut and his mates were not really having a great time.

Mark then used a time-honoured tradition among comperes as a quick way out of a developing situation: 'Please welcome your first act for the evening, Tim Smith!'

Tim went on and did what he calls 'the fastest 15-minute spot I've ever done in my life'.

He actually did quite well and most of the crowd was having a reasonable time. Mark Neal came back out and got straight back into it with crew-cut, and after a few more back and forths, Mark had had enough and shouted out to Gordon, the guy who was running the night, 'Are you going to throw this arsehole out?'

'Just keep going!' shouted Gordon from the back of the room, 'It's hilarious!'

This pissed Mark off and, possibly sensing that the night could take a turn for the worse, he said, 'Normally we'd go to a break right here but, ladies and gentlemen, here's Russell Gilbert.'

Russell went on and smashed them in the way that he does, but it was still a bit of a tough gig, even for him.

After Russell finished, they went straight to a break, and Mark walked up to the back of the room and said to Gordon, 'Well, there you go. That's the show. You didn't toss that crew-cutted dickhead out and now the show's over.'

Gordon said, 'What about "drink for a joke"?'

Mark replied 'There'll be no drinky and no jokey for those cunts tonight!'

'Yes there will be,' says Gordon, 'or there'll be no payey for Marky and Timmy and Russy tonight.'

'All right then,' said Mark. 'Let's get this over with.'

They started up the 'drink for a joke' final set and Mark could tell that crew-cut wanted to get up, but he wasn't going to make it easy for him. Mark got up a steady stream of punters to tell their jokes and most of them got a free drink for their effort. After crew-cut yelled out, 'My dead cat could tell a better joke than you,' Mark let crew-cut come up to the microphone and then he promptly went and sat in crew-cut's seat at the table of sailors.

Every time crew-cut tried to start talking, Mark just started screaming out every moronic, thick-headed line that crew-cut had shouted at him during the night. And worse. Of course crew-cut was not practised in the put-down lines like the experienced comedians were, so he was having an awful lot of trouble trying to tell his joke. The crowd was lapping it up, which only added to the humiliation that crew-cut and his mates felt.

Tim and Russell were watching all of this from the back of the room, thinking it was one of the funniest things they had seen.

Mark was in the middle of a line like, 'and another thing you stupid –' when he went silent.

Russell grabbed Tim by the arm and said, 'Mate, it's just got really serious. There's a guy about to stab Mark in the throat with a knife!'

Tim looked over and saw that one of crew-cut's mates, who was sitting next to Mark, had pulled out a knife and was holding it up against Mark's throat. It was no butter knife either, it was a proper, pointy, razor-sharp, 'that's not a knife – this is a knife' kind of a knife. The knife guy said in a threatening voice, 'Why don't you just shut the fuck up and let my mate talk!'

Russell said to Tim, 'Look, I don't think he's going to actually stab Mark, because he probably would have done it by now, so what we need to do is get the car ready and get the fuck out of here. Where are the car keys?'

'Oh shit, they're in Mark's jacket,' said Tim.

Luckily Mark wasn't wearing his jacket, it was hanging up backstage.

Russell said, 'You get the keys, go get the car and bring it around to the front entrance.'

'Righto,' said Tim.

'And leave the engine running,' said Russell.

As Tim went off to get the getaway car ready, Russell put on his best 'good bloke' face and threw himself into the fray, saying things like, 'Aw, boys, how's it going?' and 'Come on, fellas, it's all gonna be okay,' doing his best to diffuse the situation.

Thirty seconds later, Russell and Mark came bolting out of the front entrance of the pub, closely pursued by five burly, angry sailors. Tim not only had the engine running, but both passenger side doors open. Russell and Mark did flying dives into the car as Tim floored it and screamed away.

With adrenaline pumping through their veins, they counted their blessings and relived the adventure, saying how lucky Mark was to escape unharmed – until they got out of the car back in Melbourne to see the six-inch long knife slash down the back of Mark's shirt.

WHY DON'T YOU BOTH **FUCK OFF THEN?**

While we could say that heckling has fallen away in live comedy, the rise of the internet and social media has seen an increase in a more subtle, yet possibly more sinister, form of heckling – the anonymous online heckler. Most comedians have Twitter accounts so they can self-promote and show the world (or less than one per cent of the world, anyway) just how incredibly witty and clever they are by the speed with which they come up with a one-liner about something topical. Twitter also leaves them open to direct criticism, and I am not saying that's a bad thing. I call this Twitter heckling 'peckling'. Not too bad either, even if I do say so myself. Twitter – tweet – bird-sounding things – heckling – peckling. That's a logical progression if you ask me.

Celia Pacquola has had her fair share of 'peckling'. She recently received a tweet that said, *'Celia Pacquola is the comedic equivalent of a stroke, I am left feeling numb, confused and not the least bit amused'*.

I don't think the person who sent that message had actually had a stroke, though, because people who experience a stroke aren't usually known to say, 'Well, that was not amusing in the least!'

Celia doesn't usually respond to pecklers on Twitter. (See how smoothly I slipped 'peckling' into the conversation then? I just can't help but think that peckling is going to quickly make its way into the modern social media vernacular or, smernacular, as I have decided to name it.)

So as I was saying, Celia doesn't usually respond to this kind of abuse, but she found herself unable to resist when she received an insult-filled rant from a Frenchman on Twitter, which of course was written entirely in French. Celia initially didn't know the message was abusive, as she doesn't speak French, and if you don't speak French even the most vile and offensive ranting reads like it could be some of the most romantic and tender love poetry you've ever heard.

Like this: *Vous êtes un cochon puant vile et avoir de la merde pour les yeux.*

That wasn't the message that Celia received, by the way, but put it into an online translator and you will see what I mean.

Celia had a French-speaking friend translate the message for her and this is what the Frenchman said:

I hate you. You are a bitch because you have the same surname as me and whenever I put my name into a search engine, your dog face comes up. You are ugly, plus you're a faggot!

I guess it could have been worse, and the overall abusiveness of the message kind of depends on what breed of dog's face he is comparing Celia's to, but she replied to the message like this:

Hello and thank you for your message. Please excuse me, as my French is not very good but, 'Je go-fuck-yourself.'

Greg Fleet has the distinction of playing the longest-ever show at the Sit Down Comedy club in Brisbane, though the length of the show was more due to self-preservation than an adoring audience.

The day started in a familiar fashion when it comes to Fleety and some of his bad gig stories, in that he spent most of the day drinking copious amounts of alcohol. Around lunchtime, Greg had met up with an old school friend and, while he would have been aware that he had a gig on that night and should have been exercising a little restraint regarding the extra large martinis, after the third or fourth extra large martini, restraint was not being exercised. The Sit Down Comedy Club was unique in that it was located at the bottom of a large hotel, and the visiting comedians were accommodated a short elevator ride away, which made drinking large martinis and still making it to the gig rather easy.

Greg recalls thinking to himself at one point in the early evening, 'Why is there wool everywhere? All I can see is wool. What is the reason for all of this wool everywhere I look?'

Then he realised he was lying face-down on the carpet in his hotel room. He dragged himself up and looked in the mirror to see his face criss-crossed by the indentations of the carpet and realised it was time to head down to do his gig.

Ten minutes later Greg and his carpet face were onstage, doing his scheduled 40-minute set. After only a few minutes, a bloke near the front started heckling and Fleety swiftly dealt with him to the delight of the audience. Then the bloke continued to heckle and Greg let fly with a tirade of abuse that was so harsh, when he looked up from his ranting he saw the audience staring open-mouthed in shock. Fleety thought he needed to get back on track and get the audience back on his side and not just staring at him like he was some kind of raging animal.

So Greg went with the usually safe comedy bet of trying to attack what the heckler did for a job, and said to him, 'What do you do with yourself when you're not being a fuckhead at comedy shows?'

'I just got out of prison,' said the man, and Fleety could tell that he wasn't lying, nor was he trying to be funny. Fleety continued on, 'Okay, right then, and how long were you in for, prison guy?'

Prison guy answered, 'Seven years.'

Fleety thought to himself, 'Seven years ... that's probably not just for parking fines.'

Then prison guy continued, 'Yep, seven years ... and I'm gonna fucken kill you.'

Fleety thought, 'Yep, I reckon he could probably do it.'

Over the next two hours, Greg continued with the show and

WHAT, AND GIVE UP SHOWBIZ?

Greg Fleet

(James Penlidis)

he said that about one hour and 40 minutes of that time was spent simply trying to save his own life. At the beginning of the gig there had been about 200 people in the room, but by the end there were only about 30 people left, including prison guy and his table of mates. The other people in the room weren't there because it was hilarious – they were there because it was fascinating.

At times Fleety would have prison guy calmed down and he would say, 'Yeah, look, mate, I guess I started it, so no worries, okay.'

Then Greg would say, 'All right, thanks mate. I over-reacted too, we're cool then, right?' Then one of prison guy's mates would fire him up again by saying, 'Nah, fuck that! Kill the bastard!' And the situation would return to being tense and Fleety would say, 'No, no, don't kill the bastard! Let the bastard run free!' The gig finally finished up with the venue owner walking onstage to tell Fleety that he had to finish up, but only after it was established that prison guy and Fleety were friends, or at least that prison guy was not going to kill Fleety.

George Smilovici stared into the darkness that surrounded him. He held his hand in front of his face but it was too dark even to see the outline of his trembling fingers. He could feel the oxygen in the confined space diminishing with each panting breath and he could hear the muffled screams and sounds of panic coming from outside the inky blackness of his cramped location. Five minutes earlier he had been standing onstage, slaying a full house of eager punters with his clever one-liners and razor-sharp put-down lines. Now he felt sleepy as the carbon dioxide from his breath slowly began to dominate the thinning oxygen that remained in his bizarre crypt. He smiled to himself as he thought that at least he wouldn't be the first comedian to have died at a suburban Sydney pub.

A million questions floated through his mind.

How did it ever come to this?

Will they ever find my body?

Why didn't I ask to get paid in cash before the gig?

It was 1985 and George was riding high on the success of his hit comedy single 'I'm Tuff,' which had recently knocked Stevie Wonder's 'I Just Called to Say I Love You' from the number one position on the Australian pop charts. In the mid-1980s, it seemed that the Australian public just couldn't get enough of Sydney comedians releasing excerpts from their routines in the guise of singles. 'I'm Tuff' was the third Australian comedy single to top the charts in two years, following on from the success of 'Australiana' by Austen Tayshus and Rodney Rude's 'I Hate That'. Inspired by those two tracks, the Scaredies unsuccessfully attempted to cash in on the success of 'Australiana' and 'I Hate That' by releasing the somewhat less successful 'Tasmaniana' and 'I Don't Mind That', but that's another story.

George was in the middle of a sell-out national tour and this particular gig was at an enormous suburban beer barn in western Sydney. It was the type of place that usually hosted gigs by Aussie rock giants such as the Angels, Midnight Oil or the Chippendales Down Under.

George was about halfway through his set and had just finished playing a song on his beautiful Ramirez classical guitar – a very expensive instrument that was his pride and joy and accompanied him to every gig. He continued on with his routine when two scrawny, possibly substance-affected blonde girls walked into the room. Their journey to wherever they were going took them just in front of the stage, where they stopped while one of them started scrounging around in her handbag for lipstick or smack or something. They were oblivious to the fact there was a comedy show going on and it was at this point that George delivered a punchline, which elicited a big laugh from the audience. This seemed to shake one of the girls out of her trance, and as the audience's laugh died down, she looked up at George, scoffed and sarcastically said, 'Ugh, ha ha ha …'

She was literally waving a comedy red flag to the bull of a fired-up George. There he was, in the middle of his show to a sold-out crowd, all of whom were on his side and now there were a couple of dodgy looking scrags standing front and centre, just asking to be paid out on.

George retaliated in the comic vernacular of the day, which was, of course, vulgar put-down lines.

'I'm really glad you girls are here tonight,' he said. 'Because now I've got something to think of later on when I'm trying not to come.'

The audience went crazy.

The two girls gave him the finger and then quickly departed. As they were walking out George added, 'Oh, and by the way girls, when you're out in the car park whatever you do don't piss on my tyres.'

About 20 minutes later, George was performing his final piece for the night – his famous 'I'm Tuff' routine. He was killing, and the audience were joining in for all the appropriate bits.

'I'm tough,' George would say.

'How tough are ya?' the audience would scream back in unison.

'I'm so tough when I was a baby I pushed my own pram. I'm tough!'

'How tough?'

'I'm so tough, I use aftershave ... before! I'm tough!'

'How tough?'

'I'm so tough my rice bubbles are too scared to go snap, crackle, pop. They hide in the pack and go "Shhh, here he comes".'

The audience were lapping it up and every line was hitting the mark with big waves of laughter.

George delivered the next line, but this time there was no laughter and the audience had become silent. He stopped and shielded his eyes from the bright stage lights and saw that most of the audience were staring out the large glass window that took up at least half of one wall of the auditorium. A loud rumbling could be heard at the same time as numerous lights shone in through the glass wall. The lights were actually headlights. Headlights of about 30 motorcycles that were carrying about 30 mightily pissed off bikies, two of whose girlfriends had just been put in their place by one George Smilovici. The bikies were visible to everyone in the room, and as they stopped and got off their bikes, it was clear that they were angry and armed with chains, fence posts, iron bars and cricket bats.

'Fuck, I'm not that tough!' said George.

It was obvious that the bikies had not turned up for a counter meal or the meat tray raffle. They were there for one reason and one reason only – to avenge the scrags. Somewhat oddly, George's first thought was not of his own safety, nor that of the audience, but of his $5000 guitar, which he quickly grabbed, then he jumped off the front of the stage and started running towards the bar at the rear of the room. As he was halfway there, he heard an almighty crash as the bikies smashed through the side window and ten metres of glass wall came crashing to the ground amid screams from the audience, as chaos now descended on the room. People were running in all directions, shouting and panicking and looking for a way out.

WHY DON'T YOU BOTH FUCK OFF THEN?

'Where can I hide my guitar?' screamed George to the barman.

'Downstairs in one of the motel rooms,' shouted the barman, quickly ushering George behind the bar and down the stairs that led to the accommodation and rear parking lot.

George got to one of the rooms and could still hear crashing, banging and screaming coming from upstairs as he kicked the door open and slid his guitar under one of the beds, wondering what the hell he was going to do next.

The barman, who had followed him downstairs, said, 'Mate, they're coming after you. Just jump over that back fence and get out of here!'

'Where am I going to go?' asked George.

'Just fucking run, and don't stop running!' came the reply.

George set off and was just about to leap the fence when another barman came flying down the stairs shouting, 'George, stop! They're coming round the other way after you! Get back up the stairs!'

Back at the top of the stairs George was met by the manager, a large, thickset bloke with a face as white as a sheet and covered in sweat. He said, 'Mate, these blokes want to kill you.'

'Was it something I said?' asked George.

'I've got an idea for where we can hide you,' said the manager. 'Follow me.'

He quickly led George to an office, bent down and opened a wall safe that was at ground level and said, 'Get in here, they'll never find you.'

George stared at the opening of the safe, which was about a metre square and thought there was no way in the world he was going to get into that safe. He turned his head quickly at a loud smashing sound coming from out in the corridor, then got down on all fours and crawled inside.

The manager slammed the door shut and George heard the

'I'm Tuff – most of the time'
(George Smilovici)

metallic clunk of the lock sealing him inside. He could hear muffled sounds of the chaos that was still going on inside the pub as the scrag-vengeance-seeking bikies tore their way through the place looking for George. He felt around him and discovered he was surrounded by bags stuffed with thick wads of cash. Even under those harrowing circumstances, George saw the irony of a Jewish boy like himself surrounded by all that cash with nowhere to spend it.

He was locked in and relatively safe, at least from the bikies, but he wondered how he would he get out if something happened to the manager. What if the manager was the only one with the combination to the safe? What if the bikies set fire to the pub and George was entombed forever in the rubble of a suburban pub to be found in a hundred years time like a Jewish mummy, surrounded by bags of cash, or at least the charred remnants of bags of cash?

Time moved slowly for George in his vault. After what seemed like hours, but was probably only about 15 minutes, he heard the sound of sirens approaching the pub and then the sweetest sound of all: the clank of the safe being unlocked and the door swinging open.

The fresh air hit him in the face like a bikie's iron bar hitting a plate glass window. By this time the pub was a scene of absolute carnage, with broken chairs and tables, shattered glass, people nursing broken limbs and cuts being attended to by paramedics and bikies in various stages of arrest. George was interviewed by the local detectives and eventually released, but after that night, whenever he came to perform his 'I'm Tuff' routine, he always recalled the night when he wasn't *that* tough.

Hello, is anybody OUT THERE?

Performing to a small audience is a recurring theme when comedians recount bad gigs, and even though it's not a given that a small crowd equals a bad show, on most occasions, that's exactly what it means.

The job of an announcer on a commercial radio station is known to be one of the most soul-destroying, energy-sapping and self-confidence-obliterating things you can do, though I guess there are also some negative aspects.

On-air (and off-air) personnel at these stations are sacked more often than an eleventh-century Norman village.

When she was given the boot from her on-air commercial radio gig, Georgina McEncroe was feeling a little low. She described being given the boot by a commercial radio station as being a bit like being dumped by a boyfriend that you never liked anyway ... just after you'd let him fondle you. She had spent a few days feeling sorry for herself when she got a call from her agent, who suggested that she had just the perfect engagement to pull Georgina out of her rejection dejection – a 10 am stand-up gig at an outer suburban shopping centre in Forest Hill. The first thing that came into Georgina's mind was, of course, 'Suburban shopping centre, 10 in the morning – what could possibly go wrong?'

The bloke who had booked her was a really big fan and he

called her up the day before the gig to discuss the details. She was sceptical of her ability to draw many people at that time of the day and told him he should scale it down a bit and make the gig fairly low-key. He said, 'Oh, don't run yourself down like that, Georgina. You'll be great and the crowd will love you! Though if you insist, I can keep it on a small scale.'

Georgina arrived at the gig to see 400 chairs set up in front of the main stage, and when she went on to begin her set, there was a total of five people in the audience. It was okay though – the five people were spread evenly throughout the 400 chairs. A few minutes after she started, she had to compete with a woman at the Brumby's Bakery just across from the stage, who was plugging cheap hot cross buns through a distorted microphone. The hot cross bun lady won.

On the drive home, Georgina was in a thoughtful mood as she contemplated the age-old saying, 'You're only as good as your last gig.' She was listening to some of her (still employed) friends talking on the radio, which didn't help, and mulling over the unpleasant gig she had just experienced. She consoled herself with the fact that with such a small crowd at least no one had seen her. Then she received a text message from a good friend that said, 'Hey, Mum and Dad were just out at Forest Hill shopping centre getting some hot cross buns and they saw you doing a gig ...'

Tim Smith once got a call from his agent about doing a private gig for a bucks' night. 'This was after I told my agent that I just didn't want to do any more bucks' nights,' said Tim. 'I had a bad experience with the last one I did. They were horribly pissed and unbearable and there was a fight during my act, so I said no more

– which of course is why my agent was calling me about another bucks' night gig.'

She was giving Tim the hard sell and making it sound attractive. She told him that they really wanted him for the gig and that they insisted that there wasn't going to be any trouble. It was in the upstairs private room at a pub in the city and he only had to do a 15-minute set. They were going to pay $2000, and if Tim could work in a couple of jokes about the groom they would throw in a bonus. Tim finally agreed but said he was not interested in doing any jokes about the groom; he was just going to do a straightforward gig. It actually sounded fairly simple. All he had to do was rock up to the pub just before he was due to go on, do a quick 15-minute set and pick up a couple of grand for his troubles.

Tim arrived at the venue just before the scheduled starting time and walked up the stairs. At first he thought he must be in the wrong place, because the room was completely empty except for four guys sitting in a row with a microphone set up right in front of them. 'Big bucks' night,' thought Tim.

The best man walked over to Tim and motioned him outside. He said, 'Aw, yeah, sorry about the size of the crowd, mate. Look, I've been overseas for a few weeks and didn't have time to follow up on all the invites for tonight. Also, just between you and me, the groom is actually a bit of a dickhead and he hasn't got many mates. I've invited over 50 people and no one has turned up. I've got responses from people saying they would rather be run over by a truck than attend this guy's bucks' night. That's why there's only four of us here – including the buck.'

Then it got better when the best man continued, 'Yeah, mate and actually about your payment for tonight, ah, we were all going to chip in to pay you so, ah, do you reckon you could do the gig for a bit less?'

WHAT, AND GIVE UP SHOWBIZ?

Tim Smith – one finger for each of his audience members
(James Penlidis)

'There's only four of you,' said Tim.

'Actually only three,' said the best man, 'the groom doesn't count.'

Tim was beginning to regret his decision.

'Look, Tim,' he continued, 'I've got a hundred bucks, Gary can chip in a hundred too, but Mick's only got forty bucks. That's all we can offer you.'

Tim thought for a bit and said, 'Look, mate, how about don't worry about chipping in any cash. I'll just sit at the table and tell you some jokes for a while.'

And that's what he did. The best man got him a beer and he sat down and did his show with an audience of four, though it was really more like four blokes at a table listening to jokes than an actual audience. Tim later said, 'I told them some old jokes – the "frayed knot" joke, the "jam jar" joke, a quick medley of knock knock jokes, I think I even threw in "why the long face?"' So sitting around that table with three blokes plus a guy that not many people liked would have definitely been the smallest audience that I ever played to.'

By the way, I asked Tim what the 'jam jar' joke was, and he told it to me like this:

An elderly couple walk into a doctor's office. The man tells the doctor, 'Doctor, we want to have a baby.' The doctor replies, 'At your age? I don't think it's possible, but I'll give you a jar and come back in a few days with a sperm sample.' So a few days later, the old guy comes back to see the doctor and he hands over an empty jar. The doctor says, 'I was afraid of this.'

The old man replied, 'No, it's not what you think. I tried it with my left hand. I tried it with my right hand. She tried it with her left hand. She tried it with her right hand. She tried it with her teeth in. She tried it with her teeth out. But we just couldn't get the lid off the jar.'

Troy Kinne had a similar experience after turning up to a bucks' night at a house in Sunshine, which turned out to be just four blokes in a shed out the back of the house.

'Okay then,' said Troy, 'which one of you is the buck?'

'Oh, he fell asleep,' answered one of the four blokes, who was also the buck's father. 'I'll just pop up to his room and wake him up.'

He returned a few minutes later and said, 'Uh, he doesn't want to come down, so it's just the four of us.'

Troy considered bailing on the gig, but then remembered a piece of advice that comedian Dave Hughes had told him when he was just starting out.

'It doesn't matter how small an audience is, an audience of one is still an audience, and they will pass your name on to other people.'

Troy shrugged his shoulders and thought he might as well just get on with it. He was halfway through his first joke when the phone inside the house rang.

'Oh, I better get that, can you just hang on for a tick?' said the father, running back into the house. Troy stood there in awkward silence in front of the three other blokes, who were the buck's grandad, cousin and younger brother.

'Michael, it's for you!' came the faraway voice of the father from inside the house, and Troy's audience dwindled down to just two, as the buck's younger brother took off to take the phone call.

Troy decided to finish off the joke and, recalling Dave Hughes' advice about small audiences, asked the remaining two blokes, 'Do you remember my name?'

'No,' they answered in unison.

'Good,' said Troy as he walked out of the shed, got in his car and drove home.

Andy Goodone travelled up to Sydney in the heady days of the mid-1980s comedy boom when it seemed like every second pub in Sydney was putting on comedy. He scored a gig at a suburban pub in the middle of the day and soon discovered that he was the only act on the bill. He arrived at the pub and was shown to the room where the gig was. There were just two blokes sitting at the bar and no one else. In the middle of the room they had a 'stage', but it wasn't really a stage, it was about five feet high but only three feet square. You could barely stand on it. It was more of a plinth than a stage. There was no way he could imagine himself going through with the gig, but then he thought, 'Well, I'm already here, and they're going to give me $150, so I might as well just do the gig.' So he did about 20 minutes standing there on the plinth, like a go-go dancer without a cage, in front of two drunken blokes in the middle of the day. They weren't ignoring Andy, or heckling or even talking, they were just looking at him and not laughing or reacting in any way. It was a very long 20 minutes.

As a comedian you learn a lot about time and the passing of it. Sometimes an hour onstage can pass with you barely realising

HELLO, IS ANYBODY OUT THERE?

Andrew Goodone contemplating the 'good times'
(James Penlidis)

it. Other times, when you are struggling, a minute can be interminable.

When all comedians end up in hell, and I am sure that's where we will all end up, there will be a little comedy room to perform in. No one understands any of your jokes, the PA will be crap, you will be dying *and* it's a benefit gig. I can only imagine how long 20 minutes felt to Andy Goodone, standing on an oversized plinth in a suburban Sydney pub in the middle of the day in front of two blokes who might has well have been statues, doing a shit gig.

After Andy finished, the owner of the pub refused to pay him because there wasn't anyone there.

After a gig in Melbourne one night, Lawrence Mooney was talking to a woman named June who had attended many of his previous shows. She asked if Lawrence would consider coming to perform at her husband's upcoming fiftieth birthday party.

Lawrence, whose 'possible shit gig' radar was tingling, decided to hose down the enquiry. 'I'm sorry, June, I don't think I can do the gig. You've seen all my material because you come to so many gigs, and parties can be very difficult to play sometimes,' he said.

June insisted, 'Oh, but my husband is such a huge fan and it would be a really lovely surprise for him. It would make the night so special and we are happy to pay you a fee.'

She was so nice, as well as being rather insistent, so Lawrence asked a few questions about the party.

'Now, where is it going to be held?'

'We're having it at a lovely restaurant in the city,' said June.

'And how many people are going to be there?'

'Oh, just the two of us, my husband and myself,' she replied.

'Just the two of you?' asked Lawrence in disbelief.

'Well, it will be three including you!' laughed June.

'Three including me …' repeated Lawrence, 'I'm sorry June, but I just can't do it.'

The distraught look on June's face caused Lawrence to then say, 'Look, here's what we can do. You donate the money you were going to pay me to the Bushfire Appeal and I will drop by the restaurant and surprise your husband and say a quick hello. I promise at the very least to be charming and funny, take the piss out of him for a bit and then leave you two to have a lovely night, okay?'

So the plan was set.

On the night of the 'party', Lawrence got to the restaurant and texted June, who met him outside, then they went in to surprise the birthday boy. Of course it went over smashingly well. Lawrence was both charming and funny, as promised, and birthday boy was overwhelmed at the amazing surprise and when Lawrence sang 'Happy Birthday' to him, the night just couldn't have got any better. After about ten minutes, Lawrence sensed that it was time for him to move on and said, 'Ah well, great to meet you, I guess I better get going then so you two have a great rest of the night and I'll see you later.'

'Oh,' said June, surprised. 'But we've ordered dinner for you, Lawrence. I hope you like lobster!'

British comedian Simon Munnery has played to an audience of just one person. Usually a show would not go ahead with such a small crowd, but the story behind this deserves to be told.

Simon had been contacted by a man from Toronto about performing a five-week engagement as part of the Toronto

Comedy Festival. Simon, who was at the Edinburgh Fringe at the time, asked some of his mates if they'd ever heard of the Toronto Comedy Festival. No one had.

Nevertheless, flights and accommodation were paid for and when the time came, Simon found himself greeted at Toronto airport by the festival's official driver, who also happened to be the publicist, accountant, general manager and financial backer. His name was Brian and up until recently he had been an accountant, but he decided that before his thirtieth birthday he wanted to become a theatrical producer, and this festival was his first and only project. Simon Munnery was also the first and only act that he had booked.

Brian had been so intent on putting on his 'Toronto Comedy Festival' that he hired a theatre on the outskirts of Toronto that had been unused for the previous five years. He then went through the Edinburgh Fringe Festival program to find a suitable act. He liked the look of Dave Gorman's show, but Dave was busy, so he then chose Simon Munnery's show, *The League Against Tedium* which is why Simon now found himself in Toronto as the star of, and only participant in, the festival. Everything up to this point sounded to Simon like the beginning of a bizarre movie, where a wealthy weirdo with a penchant for comedy forces an artist to perform for his own entertainment in a large, decrepit theatre for five weeks. Apart from that it sounded just great.

Brian wasn't completely insane or hopeless, though – he had secured beer sponsorship for the venue, along with a couple of bar staff, and there was a stage manager and follow spot operator and the opening night had over 200 people in the theatre, which had a capacity of around 500 – not too bad. However, the audiences progressively got smaller and smaller and Simon had a matinee performance about three weeks into the run that had pre-sales of three people, but the show still went ahead. After interval, Simon came out and noticed that something was different. 'Ah yes,' he thought, 'two of the three people have gone and the audience is down to the magical number of one.' Simon was undeterred, as that one audience member continued to laugh for the rest of the show and enjoyed himself.

Simon later said that once you get over the fact that there is only one person, the performance can be just as valid and satisfying as if there were hundreds of people there.

Simon tested these small audience ideas out to the extreme with a conceptual show that he came up with that had him performing to a maximum of eight people seated around a dinner table, with himself as the waiter. There was no real food to muck around with; he advertised it as, 'All the rigmarole of haute cuisine, without the shame of eating.'

He got the idea after he had gone out to dinner and observed the 'performance' of the waiter for the 'audience' of the people sitting at his table in a restaurant.

Performing to an audience of eight people when that's all you're expecting changes your feelings about playing to a small crowd. The audience don't feel sorry for the performer that there are only eight people there, but the downside is that you have to charge two hundred bucks a ticket to make any money. Simon got around this by making the shows only 15 minutes long and doing eight shows per day.

If you're expecting an audience of a thousand, yet only eight people turn up, it is bad for a few reasons. It doesn't look good to have so many empty seats and the audience feels a bit awkward, not to mention the performer. Add to that the fact that you, or the producer, are probably losing a shitload of money having booked a thousand-seater when you can't fill it. But if you get eight people to a gig that has a capacity of eight people, it's a full house every night

The droll dude from Dalby, Greg Sullivan, tells of an early foray into sketch comedy that yielded a small crowd for him and five mates, who decided upon the 'safety in numbers' plan for doing comedy. They decided to put on a sketch comedy show in an internet café, because, they thought, what do people like more when they're checking their emails than to have some amateur sketch comedy thrust at them? Okay, maybe they didn't really think it through, but this was quite a popular internet café and usually had quite a few people in it. They had put up some posters for the gig and when the time came for them to start the show, they announced to the 35 people in the café that there was a free sketch comedy show starting and everyone was welcome to stay and enjoy the show. Immediately 34 people got up and left the café. The one person left was coincidentally someone that Greg Sullivan had gone to school with.

'So, how's that comedy career coming along, Greg?'

'Yeah, really well thanks for asking ...'

Greg and his mates decided to go ahead with the show, because after all, they had written all the sketches, and they had props. At one point, the audience member had to go to the toilet, so they just stopped in the middle of a sketch and waited until he came back. At which point they continued on with the show, though Greg was picturing the poor guy desperately trying to squeeze out of the bathroom window so he could escape.

At the end of the night, instead of them all signing the poster, they got the audience member to sign it for them.

Shows with small crowds, as you're beginning to understand, are reasonably common in the glamorous world of showbiz, especially when listed one after another in a compendium such as this. As we have learned, though, a small crowd doesn't automatically mean a bad show, just as a large crowd doesn't necessarily dictate that you're going to have a great show. We've heard about plenty of audiences of under five people, and a fair few shows have gone ahead with less than that number. But if you're looking for pure failure when it comes to empty-seat-to-audience-member ratios, then we simply can look no further than my old friend Damian Callinan.

Damian was booked for a daytime university show during the term holidays – warning bells may have rung for some people upon hearing this first piece of information, but the girl from student activities who was organising the gig assured Damian that there would be a big crowd. The audience wouldn't consist of the regular students, of course, because it was the holidays and they would all be working at Subway. This event was for the Distance Education students, in other words students coming in from regional areas to do special study programs while the regular students were asking complete strangers the question 'Six-inch or foot-long?'

The student activities girl had thought to offer a break from the rigmarole of study with the idea of a lunchtime show. Damian was a little upset when he first saw the giant banner that read 'Soup and Comedy – $2' and thought that at least it could have said 'Comedy and Soup – $2'. I mean, I've done some pretty lousy support spots in my time, but I've never supported soup. Still, 'living the dream', I guess.

To say that the student activities girl was being a little ambitious by setting up 900 chairs for the show is understating it somewhat, because no one turned up for the show. Nought, nil, nada, no one. Not even for the soup, which I believe was a delicious spiced pumpkin. At one stage the creaking sound of the door opening at the rear of the room caused Damian and the student activities girl to turn hopefully, to see if it was 900 people coming in for some soup/comedy, but it was just a young mother with a pram, looking for somewhere to breastfeed her baby. The student activities girl told Damian that he wouldn't have to perform his show and that it was the first event she had ever organised (surprise, surprise), then she burst into tears. On his way out, Damian overheard the girl saying to someone, 'I don't know what happened, they told me he was famous.'

I believe that student activities girl learned from her empty seat experience and she is now in charge of booking the crowds for domestic cricket matches at the MCG.

The final tale of tiny audiences is from a UK comedian who goes by the name of Jimbo. What Jimbo does could be described as anti-comedy – everything from free association to witty repartee, existentialist mime, or just plain unfunny nonsense. Certainly never the 'Two nuns walk into a bar' type of one-liners. He looks a bit unkempt, with wild, thinning hair, has a skittish manner and speaks with a slight stutter.

After seeing his act, some people describe him as simultaneously being the worst and best comedian they have ever seen, running the fine line between genius and madness.

Jimbo mostly plays open-mic nights and try-outs and, love him or hate him, he's obviously got the balls to get up there and be different and he couldn't give a toss. If he did get a paid gig, he would often walk straight off the stage, out the door and head directly to the train station and go home without collecting his cash. Or he would exit through a window then immediately climb in another window without his trousers on. Comedians usually speak of him with equal parts respect and disbelief.

For years his act comprised him coming onstage and messing about with the microphone stand for ten minutes without saying a word.

Jimbo once heard about a comedy competition in a Manchester pub that had a first prize of £200, so he jumped on the train from London and headed up there to try his luck.

He arrived to find Manchester in the grip of a horrendous snowstorm that had brought all transport within the city to a complete standstill. With all buses and trains cancelled, there was no way Jimbo could get to the pub, which was on the outskirts of Manchester, to compete for the prize money. Unless, of course, he walked. Two hours later, Jimbo burst through the doors of the pub, brushing snow off his shoulders and stamping his near-frozen feet. He couldn't believe he had actually made it there, and he headed to stand in front of the inviting open fire to warm his hands when he noticed that something wasn't quite right about the pub. He looked around and the venue was completely empty, save for the manager and one barmaid. They both looked at him with astonishment, as no one was even out driving in the foul weather, let alone walking through it.

'You all right there, mate?' asked the manager.

'I'm here for the comedy competition,' said Jimbo.

'Well,' said the manager, 'you're the only one who's turned up.'

'Oh,' said Jimbo, more than a bit disappointed at having travelled all that way in such discomfort.

Then the manager said 'So, I guess you're the winner then. I'll just go and get your 200 quid and you can be off!'

'Hang on a minute,' said Jimbo.

'What's wrong?' asked the manager.

'I haven't done my act yet,' said Jimbo.

'All right then,' said the manager, smiling and pointing to the stage. 'Knock yourself out.'

So Jimbo got up onstage, with no one in the audience, and did his act. When he got off stage and came over to the bar, the manager was standing there with his mouth open and said, 'I'm not paying you for that shit, get out of here! And have a nice walk back into town!'

Before we move on, let's have a look back at the small audience stories to see if we can crown a winner.

The smallest crowd I ever played for was seven people, when the Phones played at a fancy Toorak dinner party, but that is not even close. Georgie McEncroe with her five shopping centre fans was a solid effort, as were Tim Smith and Troy Kinne, with their four bucks' night attendees. Andy Goodone doing his set on a plinth to two barflies should be applauded, as should Laurence Mooney for turning up for a fan's fiftieth party at a restaurant that involved just the birthday boy and his wife – though he did score a lobster dinner out of it.

It could be argued that Damian Callinan's university show where no one turned up is the winner; though, while there was no actual audience, there were a few of the organisers in attendance. Plus, he didn't get to perform any of his show, so technically I reckon it doesn't count. So that makes the winner of the 'I had an audience of one person and actually went through with the show' a split between Greg Sullivan and his sketch group performing to one person, and Simon Munnery, who went through an entire second act with his audience of one.

We could reason that Greg's internet café gig wins due to the fact that there was a cast-to-audience-member ratio of six to one, or .16666 audience members per cast member. A case could also be made for Jimbo, who decided to perform to no one to claim first prize in the comedy competition in which he was the only entrant, and which he subsequently lost. Though the manager of the pub and the barmaid were watching, which could theoretically be described as an audience of two. However, I am going to spring on you a late entrant.

There was a gig performed by Melbourne blues vocalist and harmonica specialist Chris Wilson, when he played an entire set in a pub and there was no one there. It began with just Chris and the barman, but after one song the barman went off to the other room, leaving Chris to play the gig by, and to, himself. More a rehearsal than a gig, but at least he was getting paid for it.

Did he just say what I THINK HE SAID?

There is an old saying that goes: 'tragedy plus time equals comedy'.

I don't know how old that saying is, though the formula itself certainly has been around as long as humans have. Sure, it wasn't that funny at the time when Grug got his arm bitten off by that cave lion last summer, but oh, how they laughed about it during those long nights around the fire that winter. Tragedy plus time does not necessarily *always* equal comedy either. Just ask any comedian who's done a Jesus joke and had some God-botherer get upset about it. I guess for some people 2000 years isn't long enough.

I remember in 1986 when the *Challenger* space shuttle exploded and a few days later jokes started doing the rounds. The jokes were spread by word of mouth, but it was the first time I can remember jokes being made about a tragic event. In the 1980s, I doubt whether even commercial radio jocks would have attacked a touchy subject too quickly. These days, with the rise of social media, the 'time' factor in the simple comedy formula has virtually disappeared. It seems everyone with a Twitter account becomes a comedian at the drop of a tragedy, punching out a dubious one-liner before the body count is finalised.

I recall one morning the Scaredies were trying to think of a topical subject to use in a song that we were to perform on radio that afternoon. We were in Brisbane, about to board a flight back to Melbourne, and all we had was a fairly lame topic about Prime Minister Kevin Rudd buying a cheap ute, and the Wimbledon tennis tournament. As we were boarding the plane, I saw a scrolling news announcement that Michael Jackson had been taken to hospital, and wondered if we might be able to scratch something together about that. Of course, two hours later, when we landed in Melbourne and were taxiing in to the gate, Jacko was dead and Facebook and Twitter were going nuts with way more jokes (funny and unfunny) than we could have come up with in those two hours.

While doing something as innately simple yet complicated as trying to make people laugh, sometimes you can just say the wrong thing at the wrong time. If you choose to do material on a controversial subject, it can be amazing or horrible, depending on the delivery, the joke itself, and the personal experience of individual audience members. I still cringe at the thought of a joke we once did in a topical song about a poor young fellow who lost both his hands after an accident swinging on a basketball hoop that collapsed. In the song, we sang that before he did the slam-dunk, he said, 'Look mum, no hands …'

Lawrence Mooney did a show at the Hi-Fi Bar in Melbourne one night a few weeks after the 2002 Bali bombings. Lawrence has never shied away from touchy subjects, and good for him, but if you ask me, trying to do jokes only a short time after an attack where over 200 people died is either brave or stupid or probably both.

It's certainly not impossible to do material about a difficult subject. I heard Ross Noble do jokes about the Black Saturday bushfires which were incredibly well crafted and very funny. It helped that he had actually lost his own house in Kinglake to the fires, and that's what the jokes were about – his own situation. Of course it wouldn't have been funny if he had lost a family member, but the skill lies in finding the right angle and telling the joke in an appropriate setting.

When you're sitting around with a group of comedians and writers trying to out-joke each other, pretty much anything goes in terms of subject matter and poor taste, because everyone there knows it's a 'safe' environment and nothing will leave the room. It's also about testing boundaries, and while the subject matter itself may not be funny, the humour comes more from the *thought* of saying those inappropriate things onstage rather than the 'joke' itself. Putting some of those thoughts up on Twitter or Facebook or, God forbid, actually doing them onstage is another matter completely, and that night at the Hi-Fi Bar, Lawrence Mooney was about to get in over his head.

When he decided to include a routine about the Bali bombings, he took the approach that there were a lot of bogans involved in the attack, and his material was based around stereotypical bogan characteristics – tonight there's an angel in heaven with braided hair, and similar sorts of observations, which you might find funny if you don't call yourself a bogan or you don't personally know anyone involved in the incident.

A few minutes into the routine, Lawrence heard a little sniffing sound coming from the audience, but he continued on. Then the sniffs turned into some quiet sobs and rather than just ignore it, he said, 'Is there someone here who lost somebody in the Bali bombing?'

An upset woman's voice from near the front said, 'Yes ... I did.'

The audience gasped and you could feel the stickiness of this already sticky situation getting somewhat stickier. Lawrence, who was already wondering where he could possibly take this conversation, continued, 'Who was it?' he asked.

'She was my best friend,' came the answer.

Now Lawrence's comedian instincts took over and he thought maybe he could salvage something out of the awkward situation

Lawrence Mooney – what a nice-looking young fellow
(James Penlidis)

by using a tried and tested piece of audience participation.

'What did she do for a living?' he asked, regretting the question as it came out of his mouth.

'Nothing,' said the woman's voice, 'she was just a mother.'

There is no possible way you could ever recover from a moment like that, so Lawrence just said, 'Oh well, let's get back to the show, shall we?'

But it was too much. No one could laugh at anything now, and audience members were walking out in a constant stream. Lawrence came offstage with his head hung low and he still shudders when he recalls that night.

If talking about the Bali bombings was difficult, then consider the comedian who tried to do jokes about the Port Arthur massacre the day after 35 people had been shot and killed at the peaceful Tasmanian tourist site.

The gig was the regular Sunday afternoon 'Espy Comedy' at the Esplanade Hotel in St Kilda, where the comedians would often tackle edgy and topical subjects.

But taking on the Port Arthur massacre *the next day* was just literally too soon. There is no other way to put it. 'Crazy E' was the rather apt name of the comedian who deemed that it was not 'too soon' to try out some Port Arthur gear before even most of the horrendous details were known. What the jokes were is irrelevant, and after about five minutes of the crowd not buying into it at all, a bloke down the front yelled out, 'Aw, come on mate, that's not fair! My brother died at Port Arthur.' But if you think about it, if this guy's brother really had died at Port Arthur, do you think he would have woken up the next day and thought to himself, 'Oh, my brother's dead, maybe I'll head down to catch some comedy at the Espy this arvo'?

So it became obvious that this bloke who had called out was just taking the piss and got himself thrown out of the venue. Later on in the afternoon another comic was doing his 'C-word' routine, where he would go through all the uses of the 'C-word' and repeat it over and over to try and demystify it. Then, in the middle of the routine, from up the back of the room a bloke yelled out, 'Aw, come on mate, that's not fair, my brother's a cunt!'

Long-haired Sydney funny man Tommy Dean has long been fascinated by controversial subjects, and for his Sydney Comedy Festival show in 2011, he didn't merely throw in a few jokes about the latest disastrous news event among routines about airline food and getting stoned. Over the course of the hour-long show, he wanted to discuss in detail the way that society deals with tragedy through comedy. The main focus for his show and, not coincidentally, the most recent world tragedy at the time, was the tsunami that had just struck Japan.

Even mentioning that topic as part of a comedy routine could immediately snap an audience out of the 'I'm sitting in a comedy club feeling good and not thinking about the real world' mood that people often go to comedy shows to achieve.

One minute they're laughing at a joke about how funny dogs are and the next they're thinking, 'Oh no, please don't say something bad about all those poor people who died in Japan.' Tommy needed to tread a fine line throughout the show, and it was a gutsy effort on his part.

Before the tsunami struck, Japan had been the focus of much criticism from around the world due to their dubious whale 'research' practices, and while we're on that subject, just how much research is really going on there?

'Yep, this one's dead too! Looks like the giant harpoon through its brain might have been the cause of death. Oh well, we may as well eat it ...'

Tommy suggested that the world suddenly felt sorry for Japan, and maybe we should say to them, 'Look, we know it's been a hard time for you as a country and in this time of terrible tragedy, if it makes you feel any better, why don't you just go out and kill a few whales?'

He pointed out how, directly after the event, you could barely even say the word 'tsunami', as it had become a synonym for 'horrible tragedy'. Yet the name of every other cataclysmic, weather-based disaster was already being used by sports teams: the Storm, the Thunder, the Lightning, the Tornadoes, the Cyclones – these are all the names of teams, both professional and amateur. Following the tsunami, some bloke would have had to turn up to his mid-week indoor cricket team and say, 'Uh, guys, I don't think we should call ourselves "The 10,000 Dead Japanese" any more.' He also dealt with the media coverage of the event, the idiosyncrasies of Japanese culture, and the world's response to the disaster in the age of social media.

The show was a clever mix of actual controversial jokes

intertwined with discussion about why they were controversial and our response to them as a society – it was a brilliant idea and well performed by Tommy. The audiences were generally sophisticated enough for this kind of contentious comedy and knew what they were in for when they attended the show. However, one particular night, Tommy immediately noticed there was something going on in the crowd that was different to the usual audience responses. There was laughter and horror; there was concern, and strange pauses that he just couldn't quite put his finger on. About a third of the way through the show he stopped and said, 'Okay, this is weird. What's going on out there tonight?'

After a longish pause someone said, 'I don't think you realise that most of the audience tonight is a group from Toshiba ...'

Yes, most of the crowd were from the Australian division of Toshiba, including, right in the front row, the Japanese head of the company, sitting with his senior management team. Tommy apologised to the head Toshiba man, but rightly backed himself and explained that he obviously wasn't trying to rub it in their faces and make fun of the tragedy, and this was taken well by everybody. To get back on track with the show, he said, 'Well, while we're all talking openly and honestly I better tell you that at the end of the show I'm going to talk about 9/11, so is there anybody here from New York?'

The crowd went crazy, as the number two Toshiba man, sitting right down the front next to the Japanese boss, was an American from New York.

Stand-up Greg Sullivan was headlining a Brisbane club on a busy Saturday night, with a packed house of about 300 people.

In that particular club a few long tables are set up to run right up to the front of the room at stage height, and as Greg came out onto the stage, he noticed a very large birthday cake, covered in profiteroles, about a metre away from the stage and visible to everyone in the room. Before he had a chance to get settled in with a few jokes under his belt, a bloke sitting next to the cake plucked off a profiterole and offered it Greg saying,

'You want one, mate?'

Greg, who is of largish stature said, 'Look at me, of course I fucking want one! But I won't because I am a bit busy up here trying to start my set.'

Then a couple of idiots yelled out simultaneously from opposite sides of the room and Greg spent just a tad too long trying to deal with them, which didn't get things off to a good start. He could sense a feeling in the room, a feeling familiar to most comedians, of the crowd becoming a little anxious that he hadn't gotten a laugh yet, so he said, 'Don't worry folks, there will be some jokes.'

Profiterole man said, 'Jesus, hurry up!'

Greg replied, 'Why? Do you have somewhere to go, mate? Is there someone on the other side of town waiting for a really angry bloke to turn up?'

That got a good laugh and Greg was off and running. In a few more minutes he finally had the crowd, though he had lost profiterole man, who eventually stood up and stormed out of the room. That gave Greg a view of a woman who was seated next to profiterole man, texting away on her phone, blissfully unaware that Greg and the rest of the audience were now looking straight at her. He continued on with his routine until he heard the woman actually start talking on her phone – one metre away from the stage.

'Look,' he said to the woman, 'I don't mind if you don't like the show and you're not having a good time, that's fine with me. But there's a whole world outside that door where you can talk and text and not have a good time – all for free. There are chairs and drinks and probably cakes like the big one in front of you, so why don't you do us all a favour and go there.'

Greg was feeling rather pleased with himself about his clever and subtle put-down line.

The woman shouted out in a loud voice that the whole room could hear, 'I had a miscarriage yesterday!'

Greg was not feeling so pleased with himself now. This was about ten minutes into his supposed 40-minute headline set. It was going to be a long half hour.

Greg said to the rest of the crowd, 'Ah, I guess we should just finish this conversation up right now, then, because it's kind of killing the comedy vibe a bit isn't it?'

Then a bloke in the audience shouted at Greg, 'Harden up!'

Greg said, 'Oh, okay then, I'll just put aside my selfish feelings of humanity towards this woman and her tragedy and continue on with the dick jokes, shall I?'

Half of the audience went 'Yeah!' so Greg had no choice but to try to continue on with some jokes, until the woman interrupted again by yelling out, to no one in particular, 'I had a miscarriage yesterday... on my birthday!'

'That explains the cake then,' Greg thought, but he had no idea what on earth he could possibly say or do that could turn this situation into some semblance of a comedy show without upsetting anybody. The room was hushed. The entire crowd was thinking the same thing as Greg – what happens now? Then a bloke right across on the other side of the room started quietly singing, 'Happy birthday to you...' and everyone joined in.

Another time, Greg was onstage at the Comedy Store in Sydney doing his routine about the fact that he had recently moved to the north coast hippy haven of Byron Bay.

'I guess deep down I'm a bit of a hippy,' he said. 'People ask me if I am a pacifist, and I tell them that pacifists seem to go to a lot of rallies and marches and get pepper sprayed – I'm what you would call a coward.'

He continued, 'But I actually do think it's a good thing to have an army. If there are people in a society who are comfortable with the idea of shooting people as part of their job, then I think it's a good idea that they are all dressed the same. Then at least we know who they are.'

The routine was going down well, and he launched into the finale:

'But I believe that Australians shouldn't be fighting and getting killed over there in Afghanistan, though I have noticed that it's only our really good guys that are the ones being killed. Every time that happens, there are many stories in the paper and on the news about how the bloke who died was a great guy and everyone loved him and he was the captain of the footy team. I've got nothing against soldiers; some of my old friends are soldiers. But soldiers are a large group of people and I just think that statistically, some of them must be fuckwits. Why don't any of the dickheads ever get killed? Just once you think you would open the paper and see, *Corporal Smith was killed today ... thank fuck for that! Nobody liked him.*'

The gig went quite well for Greg that night, until he got offstage and the other comedians said to him, 'Hey, Greg, there's ah ... a rather large man out in the foyer who would like to have a quick word with you about some of your political views.'

Greg went out and met a giant of a man who was a special ops soldier, recently returned from Afghanistan. He said to Greg, 'Look, mate, last week I lost a good mate over there and you shouldn't say that kind of stuff.'

'I didn't mean to upset you,' Greg said to the towering soldier, 'and please remember that during my act I said I was a coward, it's true. Look, do you want to sit down and have a chat about it?'

Greg could see the man was struggling internally, possibly trying to restrain himself from killing Greg with his bare hands, though he seemed to be doing an okay job of not killing him. Finally the soldier mumbled, 'Oh, fuck this,' and wandered back into the room.

This got Greg thinking about the effect material about controversial subjects has on people. He really liked the routine, but was it worth hurting people like that?

Greg Fleet was smashing the crowd one night when he launched into his very funny shark attack routine that goes: 'You know that some people say that when your leg gets bitten off by a shark, you don't even know that it's happened. I find that pretty hard to believe – surely you would notice after a few days. "Gee, I'm leaning fairly heavily to the left here."'

The crowd was going off when he noticed a couple crying in the second row. He stopped the show mid-laugh (first mistake) and asked the couple if they'd had an experience with a shark attack (second mistake).

The man explained sadly that they had lost their 13-year-old son in a shark attack. Talk about a way to kill the vibe. Fleety was lost for words, then said the first thing that came into his head (third mistake), which was, 'Oh well, maybe the shark has taken your son to a better place ...' he paused for a second, '... like Hawaii.'

The Umbilical Brothers were performing in Austin, Texas on 12 September 2001 – the night after the attack on the World Trade Center. Five minutes before the curtain was about to go up for start of the show, the theatre manager came back stage to tell them that there would be two minutes' silence before the show started. As David and Shane stood there, wondering how that would affect the audience, Dave suddenly noticed that the 6 × 4 metre backdrop that the Umbies were using depicted a huge brick wall with a massive explosion painted on it – probably not the best thing to be staring at for two minutes while contemplating the attacks on the World Trade Center.

Needless to say, the show was held back a bit while they hastily covered up the backdrop.

Lano and Woodley's Colin Lane was appearing as a guest on the live stage version of *Pictures of You*, a show that features famous people sharing stories based around childhood photos. It's a bit like *The Voice* – except they use celebrities and not undiscovered singers, and they talk about photos instead of singing weird cover versions of well-known songs. Actually, it's nothing like *The Voice*.

Colin was in the middle of his spot and was chatting away to the host – amiable ex-avant-garde poet Brian Nankervis – about one of the photos that he had brought along. It was a photo from a summer birthday party in the early 1970s in Perth, where Colin grew up. It featured several ten year olds wearing awkward Seventies party clothes, gathered around a birthday cake, with Colin's mother standing to one side. Colin described to the audience how his mother was a keen sunbather who would get a very dark tan during the summer months. He then joked about how more people would have been attending the party but they cancelled when they found out his mother would be doing a 'black-face' routine, which of course wasn't true. The joke got a mixed reaction, so Colin said, 'Well that didn't sound as funny as I thought it was going to be,' which got a bigger laugh and everything seemed fine again.

Colin and Brian were about to go on with the show when a dark-skinned woman in the audience yelled out, 'Well, you've got a white face,' which was meant to be funny, but sounded a little bit weird given what had gone before it. Now, because of the bright stage lights, Colin didn't know that the woman was black, and he said, 'Where are you, I can't see you?' which elicited an audible gasp from the surrounding audience members. The woman said, 'Well, you can't see me, because I'm black.' Colin froze. Nothing puts a damper on a light-hearted conversation about family photos like a bit of racial tension. The gig could have turned a bit ugly from that point, but her comment was actually said in a friendly way, though I reckon they got onto the next slide pretty quickly.

In mid-1996, the Scaredies were in the middle of a three-month tour across the United States when we did our bit for Australo-Afro-Americano relations.

We had just completed three days in Los Angeles and the next gig was in Chicago. That would seem fairly straightforward in the logistical department, but not for our frequent-flyer-loving agent, who was known for programming gigs at ridiculously long distances from each other. Like the time he had us doing four shows in three days, driving over 2000 kilometres across five states of the US, during which time we hit a deer on the interstate at two in the morning, wrecked our rental car and played a show on the back of a truck to 15 people in a football field. Good times ...

On this occasion, instead of flying directly to Chicago from LA, we were to fly from LA back to Orlando, Florida, where we had begun our journey, and therefore use the (cheaper) return airfare. When I pointed out that only left us with a short 18-hour drive from Orlando to Chicago, our agent noted that the flight was via Atlanta, Georgia, and that we could get off the plane there, pick up a rental car and then start the drive to Chicago, slicing a cool six hours off the drive. I still wasn't sold on the idea, so he sweetened the deal with the offer of cutting the drive in half and stopping for the night in Louisville, Kentucky. He said that he could probably even get us a spot at a local comedy club in Louisville. That didn't sound too bad – even a bit fun.

The problems began at check-in at Los Angeles. To get off the plane with all of our luggage in Atlanta, instead of Orlando, we had to use the kerbside check-in system that was common in the United States before security was stepped up after 9/11. We didn't realise that you had to tip the check-in guy ten bucks per bag then whisper something like, 'The peach trees are lovely this time of year in Atlanta,' while winking, so that he would then tag the bags to Atlanta for you, instead of your ticketed destination. We just rolled up to the check-in desk at the terminal before being told that we had to travel through to Orlando, then realised that we of course faced the extra six hours of driving. When we got to Orlando I called our agent who asked incredulously, 'Why didn't you get off the plane in Atlanta?'

'Ah, because no one told us you had to grease the palm of the kerbside check-in guy,' I said.

'But everybody knows that!' he said, laughing.

'Apparently not,' I said, not laughing.

'Well now you guys have an extra six hours of driving, you better get going.'

Needless to say, we were running late when we arrived at the

Comedy Caravan in Louisville, but it wasn't so bad, as we were to be the last act on the bill that night. Due to our hectic travel arrangements, it was the only chance we would have to play in Louisville, and our agent had pulled a favour with the club owner to get us a spot at late notice. We had played heaps of similar comedy clubs to this one, and we knew we would slot right in just fine, unless of course it was the first night of Black History Month, which it was, and they were hosting a special 'All African-American line-up of comedians', in which case we would stand out like, well, like a pair of young Aussie white-boys in matching outfits, singing gently amusing country/folk tunes.

I consider myself to be an open-minded, honest person who is colour-blind when it comes to relating to other human beings, and I have travelled extensively through the south of the USA and met many African-American people and had many great times and good conversations. But I found going onstage as the final of ten acts, all of whom were black, in front of a predominately black audience and being introduced as 'two little white Aussies' to be a rather intimidating experience. All the comedians who had been on before us were standing with folded arms near the bar. We came onstage, and from the back of the room a deep voice said, 'What y'all doin' here?' which scared the absolute crap out of John and me. There was a pause and I fought off the impulse to say, 'Where da white women at?'

Instead, I leant forward to the microphone and said in the strongest accent I could muster, 'Ah, g'day,' which broke the ice and got a huge reaction from the crowd.

I don't think the audience knew quite what to make of us, or how to understand us, as we were talking rather quickly. The turning point came when we did our version of Prince's song 'Kiss', where we would solicit audience requests for different styles of music to perform the song in. The first one called out was 'reggae', which stormed it, and we closed with our rap version. To think that I had been intimidated before! Performing a comedy rap version of 'Kiss' to that room made my heart beat out of my chest. I looked over and saw the comedians all high-fiving each other and doubling up with laughter, and I can only imagine how ridiculous it must have looked to them.

After the gig and following some rather awkward attempts at handshaking and high fiving, we spent some lovely time meeting the other comedians and 'hanging out', which means 'meeting the other comedians'. After a few beers, one of our new friends, whose name was Tyrone, said, 'So, I hear y'all been kicking them Aborigines' asses over there in Australia.'

Everyone was silent.

'Um,' I said, 'yes, there have been some difficult issues involving our Indigenous Australians, and if any of you pussies have got a problem with it maybe I'll just have to kick y'all asses too!'

I didn't really say that last bit, but after I assured our new friends that neither John nor myself were in any way involved in the 'kicking of the Aborigines' asses' we continued on well into the night with our new homies.

You think you're funny, mate? Prove it! But what if you had to prove it in court?

The side-burned satirist from Sydney, Dave Bloustien, is known for tackling political subjects in his comedy routines, and not long after the racially motivated riots in Cronulla occurred, he was including a fair amount of material on that touchy subject.

He was contacted by a youthful-sounding event manager who specialised in putting on events for high schools. When the promoter, whose name was Sam, phoned Dave, he said that he had seen him perform and thought he would be perfect for an upcoming high school formal he was organising on a harbour cruise around Sydney Harbour. The reason he thought that Dave would be perfect for the gig is that the high school was from the Cronulla area. Maybe Sam thought that some of the students had been directly involved in the riots and would enjoy hearing discerning comedy material about the social undercurrents that inspired such unrest. Or maybe not.

After hearing the details of the gig, Dave's bad gig radar was tingling, so he quoted a price that he was sure would be too high for a high school formal – $2000 – therefore ensuring that he wouldn't have to do the gig. To Dave's surprise, Sam agreed and asked him to come in to his office the following day for a briefing with the all-important school formal committee.

Things started a bit weirdly when Dave arrived at Sam's office to find him hiding behind a desk in the corner of the room.

'What are you doing?' asked Dave, puzzled.

'Oh, sorry,' Sam said, emerging from his hiding place and dusting himself off. 'I just fired my graphic designer and I thought you were him.' A statement that raised more questions than it answered.

The school formal committee arrived, which consisted of three uppity Year 12 girls, and they revealed the subtle plans that would ensure the success of the formal, which was basically getting Dave to bully as many of the other students as possible by giving him personal information about them to use in his routine – including the fact that several of the girls had got pregnant that year.

He told them that surely, as this was one of the last times all of them would ever be together socially, they would just want to be chatting and dancing and not hearing a comedian make jokes about how some of them had got up the duff, so he definitely wouldn't be mentioning that.

'So, are there any unwed teenage mothers in the audience tonight?'
Not a good idea.

Sam was insistent that the comedy spot would work, and he was so sure it was going to go well he convinced Dave that two separate spots would be the best way to go.

On the night of the high school formal harbour cruise spectacular, nothing was on Dave's side. There was no room on the stage, he was jammed next to the DJ booth, there was no stage lighting to speak of, and instead of being introduced as Dave Bloustien, the emcee said, 'Please welcome Daniel Brewster!' He started by trying out some of his regular material, which got nothing, so he started to do his routine about the Cronulla riots, which he said drew smiles from the audience, but might have been a little heavy for a crowd of 17 year olds. He decided to move on to another subject and, as Dave's baby daughter had just been born and he had a routine about babies, without giving it a second thought he said, 'Okay then, here's a subject that some of you might relate to ...'

If awkward squirms were an indication of an audience loving a performer, then Dave absolutely killed. Five minutes later, he got off 'stage' and searched for Sam the promoter. Dave eventually found him hiding behind a curtain in the galley. I'm kidding – there were no curtains on the boat: he was hiding behind a lifeboat. Dave told him that it was a disaster and that comedy was just not working for this crowd.

'But you've got to do your second set,' insisted Sam.

Reluctantly, Dave went back on for a second disastrous set, then finally the pain was over – or so he thought. There was no backstage area and the cruise still had two hours to go, so he was faced with a steady procession of high school students who disliked him walking past him for the rest of the night.

After the gig, Dave wrote a long email to Sam. He made several positive suggestions that he thought might improve any similar gigs that Sam might put on in the future, including not booking Dave ever again, and even suggested other comedians who might be better suited for the gig. He included an invoice for his fee, which he generously halved to $1000, then sat back and waited for a reply, but none came. Over the next few months, Dave called and left messages and sent more emails, but Sam was hiding from him behind the metaphoric 'curtain' of cyberspace. They had only had a verbal contract and, upon receiving legal advice, Dave then went through the lengthy process of sending a letter of demand, then a hand-delivered court summons setting a date in court – which Sam did not turn up for, so Dave won by default. Then he had to try and actually get some money out of Sam, so he had a sheriff go around to visit, which didn't work. I wonder if he checked behind the curtain?

Then Dave received a letter from Sam's lawyer stating that they never received the invoice or the court summons, and not only would they have turned up for court, but they would have countersued on the grounds that Dave was in breach of contract because he was employed as a comedian and that implies that he would be funny. As he was not funny, he was therefore in breach of contract.

Another court date was set, and Dave set about writing a long letter of defence, which he submitted to the court, to prove that he was funny. He wrote a 14-page document that included a CV, reviews and jokes he had written for *Good News Week* and *The Glass House*. On the day of the second court appearance, a full 18 months after the date of the gig, Sam still didn't turn up, but his lawyer did. He declared on Sam's behalf that they had no answer to the extensive proof Dave had provided that he was funny, therefore Dave won the case. Again.

The next day, as Dave was celebrating his moral and financial victory, he received news that Sam and his company had filed for bankruptcy because they were being sued by the Salvation Army for $10,000, so there was no chance of Dave ever getting paid anyway. At least he had a moral victory to celebrate.

We don't like your kind ROUND HERE

I love playing shows away from big cities. Call it what you want – the bush, the boondocks, the backwoods, or, to some people, 'hell' – shows performed in little old country halls, mechanics institutes or quaint rural theatres have been some of my favourite shows. The Scaredies did many tours around the country with the assistance of Regional Arts Australia, an excellent organisation which works with local groups to put on shows in country towns that might not otherwise be able to host entertainment other than the odd gumboot-throwing competition or cowpat bingo at the local church fete.

Don't get me wrong – I enjoy a good sheep-shearing event as much as the next bloke, unless that bloke is Jackie Howe, in which case I enjoy it slightly less than the next bloke, but when city slicker comedians get out in the country once and a while and do a bit of touring, it can be quite entertaining.

Rod Quantock was at the end of a tour through regional Victoria, when he had an interesting cake-related incident involving a passionfruit sponge. During the publicity run before the tour started, Rod did the usual radio and press interviews with regional stations. When it came to giving out the ticketing information for each gig, he would always add that anyone who brought along a passionfruit sponge cake would get in for free. The tour progressed and to Rod's disappointment, no passionfruit sponges were brought along. On the night of the final show of the tour, he arrived at the quaint country hall of the small town that was the venue for the gig, and was met by the woman in charge. Her name was Irene and, much to Rod's delight, she was holding a magnificent passionfruit sponge cake.

'Irene, you shouldn't have,' said Rod, lying.

'Oh, it wasn't much trouble,' said Irene, in the calm, no-bullshit manner that many of Australia's excellent countrywomen possess.

She had likely got up at 5 am that morning, milked the cows, raised five children, done the accounts, prepared breakfast, lunch and dinner for her husband, knackered a sheep, killed a snake *and* found the time to bake a passionfruit sponge cake that was so light and delicious it would have stiffened Matt Preston's cravat.

It was easily the tastiest-looking passionfruit sponge cake that Rod had ever seen, smelled or had the pleasure of standing in close proximity to.

'By the way,' said Irene, 'this cake is for the raffle tonight, so if you want it, you're going to have to win it.'

'But I've never won a raffle in my entire life,' said a disappointed Rod.

Irene said, 'Well, the tickets are five for a dollar and you've got to be in it to win it!'

Ever the good sport, Rod bought a dollar's worth of tickets and wrote his name on each of the ticket stubs, as is the standard procedure in small-town cake raffles.

When it came time for the raffle to be drawn, Rod mounted the stage armed with a bucket of ticket stubs with names written on them, and did a suitable building up of tension. Nothing focuses a crowd in a small country hall like the drawing of a passionfruit sponge cake raffle. When he had the attention of everyone in the room, Rod drew the first ticket out and read the name to himself – 'Rod Quantock' was the name written on the ticket. He had won! For a split second his heart leapt at the realisation that the sponge cake was his, but Rod paused and said nothing. He was an experienced professional after all, and he knew better than to read out his own name as the winner of a small town sponge cake raffle, so he quickly crumpled up the winning ticket with his name on it and put it in his pocket. He drew out another ticket and read the winner's name. Again the ticket said 'Rod Quantock'. 'This is ridiculous,' he thought. There must have been over 300 tickets in that bucket, just five of which had his name written on them and he had just pulled out two of them on his first two goes. Again he crumpled up the ticket and put it into his pocket. Third time lucky, Rod pulled another ticket out of the bucket and read – you guessed it – his own name. This happened two more times before Rod realised that every one of the 300 tickets in the bucket had his name written on it. Irene had planned the whole thing for weeks, and the plan succeeded perfectly.

One night after a show in the middle of regional New South Wales, the Scaredies and our sharp-witted soundman, Glen, were driving back to our motel when we took a wrong turn. It wasn't a bad wrong turn, though, as we soon realised we were still travelling in the correct direction, only on a back road that was parallel to the one we wanted. It's interesting how an inadvertent wrong turn in a small town can suddenly turn into an unexpected adventure. On one side of the street we were now driving on was a neat row of houses with tidy gardens, and all of these houses faced a large cemetery with a rusty iron fence on the opposite side of the road. As we neared the turnoff to get back to the motel, the headlights of our van illuminated a cat that was playing with something underneath a parked car. We drove closer and saw that the object of the cat's attention was a rather large snake and, judging by its stripes, it was a rather large and venomous tiger snake.

'That is one big fucking snake!' said the ever-observant Glen. 'I wouldn't want to come out and find that bastard under my car,' he continued.

That made us think a little about what, if anything, we should do about the snake. John, who was driving, stopped the car and said, 'Maybe we should tell the people in the house about the snake, in case they come out and disturb it while getting into their car.'

I said, 'It's probably just made its way over from the cemetery and if we leave it alone, it will just go back over there once it has bitten and killed that stupid cat that keeps annoying it.'

Glen joined in, 'Actually, I think we really should tell those people in that house about the snake, it would be the right thing to do.'

I don't know what happened between the theatre and the snake, but I suddenly felt like I was in an episode of Thorpie's *Undercover Angels*.

'It's 10 o'clock on a Sunday night, just leave the poor snake alone and it will go away,' I said, not really caring either way as long as I didn't have to get out and talk to a stranger about the large tiger snake under their car.

Ever the well-intentioned one, John said, 'I'm going in.'

The sound of a knock on your door at 10 pm is rarely going to be good news. A knock on your door at 10 pm on a Sunday night in a small country town happens fewer times a year than a decent gumboot-throwing event, and that was why, when the door opened, John was met by a man wearing pyjamas and holding a gun. Not a big gun, probably more of an air rifle than a gun actually, but it had the wooden handle and black metal barrel that, to city boys like us, looked quite scary.

'What?' said the man gruffly.

'Uh, er ... oh,' John was a little startled and could only spit out the words, 'snake', 'cat' and 'car' while gesturing in the general vicinity of the street, as a warm, wet patch slowly materialised down his thigh. John swears that last bit didn't really happen, though he was wearing black trousers, so it was difficult to really tell.

The man looked suspiciously out to the street to see Glen and me pointing furiously in the direction of the snake-cat-car, like two terrified wusses who didn't want to be mistakenly shot by a man wearing pyjamas.

He put his gun down and said, 'Righto, let's have a look then,' while grabbing a torch on his way out to the car.

'That is one big fucken tiger snake,' said scary pyjama man.

'That's exactly what I said,' said Glen, giggling, though his giggling ceased with a quick deadpan look from pyjama man, who then said, 'I reckon he's crawled over here from the cemetery.'

'That's exactly what Rusty said,' Glen observed with a little less giggling, which ceased altogether under the combined glares of pyjama man and myself.

'So what do you reckon we should do, mate?' I said with a voice about an octave lower than my usual speaking voice. It was the kind of voice that blokes put on when they are asking other, far more experienced blokes what they reckon you should do. I use that voice when I'm talking to visiting tradesmen, blokes who work in hardware stores, and scary blokes in pyjamas who answer the door holding rifles.

'Here's what we'll do,' he said.

We all listened intently.

'I'll get the hose and you stand back over there,' he said to John. Then he looked at me, 'And you hold the torch.' My deep-voiced enquiry had obviously made quite an impression on him, as I had been given the very important job of 'torch holder'. He ignored Glen.

'I'll just spray the bastard with the hose and he'll go back across the road,' said pyjama man, who then turned on the hose, which immediately sprayed in all directions, soaking his pyjamas. He let off a colourful stream of swear words as he narrowed the jet of water, then concentrated on squirting the snake from underneath his car. It sounded like a good plan, and let me tell you I held onto that torch with extreme concentration, using both hands. The plan was not a good plan though, as the snake merely got irritated and looked for the easiest way out, which was to wind its way up the inside of the wheel and into the chassis of the car.

There was a pause of about ten seconds as we stood there in silence, the only sound being the steady drip … drip … drip of water falling from pyjama man's wet pyjamas. We took that as our cue to say, 'Oh well, I guess we've done all we can here, good night, pyjama man.' We promptly jumped into our van and headed back to the motel. As we were unloading our gear, I saw the motel owner and told him our story. He gave me a business card for the local snake removal man, which had printed on it: *All hours, night and day! Give us a call!*

As far as I was concerned, 11 pm on a Sunday night definitely qualified as 'all hours night and day', so I gave him a call and passed on the address of the angry tiger snake hidden in a car. I hoped he liked challenges, as this was surely going to test him.

As John, Glen and I went off to our separate rooms to retire, I couldn't help thinking about poor old pyjama man. All he probably wanted from his Sunday night was to sit down in his comfy chair and watch *McLeod's Daughters* while nursing his favourite firearm. Now, not only had he been disturbed by three do-gooder knuckleheads, his pyjamas were soaked and he also had a wet, extremely pissed-off tiger snake hiding somewhere inside his car. Oh, and a $150 call-out bill to the snake removal man – it was late on a Sunday night, after all.

When you're standing up on-stage, most times, due to the bright stage lights, it really is quite difficult to see anything, or anyone, in the audience. Personally I always prefer complete darkness in the crowd and have always been a little uncomfortable during a daytime show where I can see people's faces. In the middle of a gig in the country, Josh Thomas once asked a large man in the front row what his name was and he replied, 'Mandy.' Josh thought the man had given him a fake name and said, 'Come on, this isn't a Boost Juice, where you can give any old fake name, what's your real name?'

'Mandy,' came the answer again.

Josh said, 'Either you're giving me a fake name or you're a big ugly woman –' The words were just out of his mouth when he realised that Mandy was indeed a woman. Hmm, just a bit awkward there – lucky Josh is good at awkward.

In the early days of mobile telephones, when a phone rang during a gig it was like some kind of special event, although an unpopular special event, as the crowd, and not the comedian, would usually deal with the situation themselves. Shouts of 'Wanker!' and 'Turn it off, yuppie fuckwit!' would fill the room, putting the person in their place and easing the minds of the rest of the crowd who, while voicing their displeasure at the person with the phone, were probably also just a touch jealous.

Even though Australians are now among the highest users of mobile phones in the world, it took many years before owning and using a mobile phone didn't give you the stigma of being a wanker.

I mean, how dare someone have a piece of the latest technology that is both convenient and useful, right?

Apart from being the size of a large dictionary, in the beginning mobile phones were used only by tradesmen and wankers. I remember a comedian walking into the dressing room of the Last Laugh with what looked like a black shoebox clipped on his belt, to the ridicule of everyone in the room.

'I need this in case someone calls me for a gig,' he protested, but all I could think was, 'What a fucking tosspot.'

Australia's most successful Egyptian comedian, Akmal Saleh, has taken advantage of his recent success, with steady regional touring around Australia. He was in the middle of a string of dates around central New South Wales when a mobile phone incident gave him an unexpected run-in with an angry New Zealander.

A few minutes into Akmal's performance in the RSL of a medium-sized New England town, two teenage girls in the front row were giggling and texting on one of their mobile phones. Akmal grabbed the phone off them and thought it would be a great idea to call someone at random from the address book in the phone. It's a nice idea that can be quite funny, depending on who you call.

Akmal was scrolling through the girl's address book and spied the name of someone called 'Kiwi'.

He asked the crowd, 'What do you reckon we give this Kiwi a call?'

'Yeah!' shouted the crowd, a few of them laughing.

Akmal didn't know that most of the crowd knew exactly who Kiwi was, and that if Akmal called him, there was probably going to be an 'entertaining' outcome.

Akmal dialled Kiwi's phone number. Actually, because phones are getting smarter and humans are getting stupider, he just touched Kiwi's name and it connected him automatically.

The phone answered and Akmal said, 'Ah g'day, Kiwi, how are you going, mate?'

Akmal had the phone on the speaker setting and was holding it up to the microphone so everyone in the audience could hear the conversation.

There was a pause and the voice said coldly, 'Akmal, is that you?' Kiwi would have known that the girls were at the show that night, and he had worked out who was calling pretty quickly, so Akmal thought, 'Okay, great, he knows me, so we can have a little fun here.'

'So, Kiwi, what are you doing tonight? Why didn't you come down to the show, you big wanker?' Akmal said, which caused a great reaction from the audience. When the laughter subsided, Kiwi said in a serious tone, 'What did you call me?'

Akmal thought Kiwi was joking, so he continued baiting him, saying things like, 'Come on Kiwi, I'll take you,' and, 'What are you going to do about it, Kiwi?'

What Akmal didn't know was that Kiwi had been recently released from prison. He had been suffering psychological problems and had been banned from playing rugby league in all of New South Wales and Queensland for being too aggressive ... This guy was too aggressive for rugby league! And Akmal had just challenged him to a fight.

The first sign that there was going to be trouble was when Akmal got offstage and there were two policemen waiting for him. They had received a call from the bouncers of the venue saying that Kiwi had shown up, and they were scared. Let's just let that sink in for a little bit. Kiwi had shown up at the RSL and the bouncers were scared. To quote Kenny Rogers, '... *and there were three of them ...*'

Kiwi was well-known to the local cops, so they thought they should head down and give Akmal a bit of a heads-up. When the cops turned up, Kiwi went away and hid in the bushes, so the cops went away and then of course Kiwi came back. Again he hung around outside the front entrance to the RSL, waiting for Akmal, so the cops were called again and the disappearing act continued.

The third time Kiwi turned up and started hanging around, Akmal called the local cop station himself. When he said, 'Hi, it's Akmal here,' the cop on the phone started laughing and said, 'Oh, mate, of all the phone numbers you could have chosen, you really picked the wrong one.'

Luckily, Akmal and his tour manager had not yet checked into a motel, though as there were only three possible motels in town, Akmal was concerned that Kiwi would try to track him down. The policeman advised Akmal that maybe they should just drive out of town a bit before choosing somewhere to stay.

They got in the car and drove without stopping to Tamworth – four hours away.

Tommy Little and Lawrence Mooney were doing a gig on a rainy night in Castlemaine in regional Victoria. It was in one of those quaint little country halls that are usually just such a pleasure to play in. They were met by Jenny, the organiser of the gig, who had charmingly decorated the hall with tables set with checked tablecloths, delightful flower arrangements and tea light candles. As is common to these types of gigs in small country halls, the audience could bring along 'supper', which would usually consist of cheese platters, dips, tiny triangular curried egg sandwiches and homemade sponge cakes of such unbelievable fluffiness and quality they just made you want to say, 'Fuck me! That's a ridiculously good sponge cake!' If you ever find yourself at one of these types of events in the country, here's a word of advice – it's best not to say 'Fuck me! That's a ridiculously good sponge cake!' in the cake-maker's face, or at least leave the 'fuck me' part out. Screaming words to the effect of, 'Oh, I could rub this cake all over my nipples and never desire sex ever again,' into the face of an elderly Country Women's Association member will not go down well, nor does it give the sponge cake the recognition it really deserves.

The gig would have been fine, apart from the fact that there were only ten people in the audience, and while Lawrence and Tommy were being paid and were happy to do the show to just ten people and their cheese platters, Jenny the show organiser was starting to panic. She finally said to the boys in a moment of excitement, 'I've got it! I'm just running down to the pub!'

Lawrence and Tommy wondered if Jenny was going to the pub to drum up some business for the comedy night, or simply to drain half a dozen pots to take the edge off her concern at the lack of audience members.

Five minutes later about a hundred excited and happy patrons from the pub came streaming in through the doors, led by Jenny, on the promise of a free comedy show and a cheese platter. It was going to be a great night after all, and what a story! At least that's what would have happened if they were in a scene from some jingoistic Australian movie, but unfortunately they were not.

What actually happened was that five minutes after running down to the pub in the rain, a soaking wet Jenny burst back through the doors and announced, 'We're all going down to the pub to do the show! There's a fiftieth birthday party going on there, and they're happy to have some comedy!' she continued excitedly.

So Lawrence and Tommy, along with the ten cheese-platter-carrying guests and Jenny, traipsed down to the local pub in the pouring rain. What Jenny failed to tell them was that the fiftieth birthday party had taken over the entire pub and it was also a fancy dress party. She also hadn't asked the birthday boy if he wanted a comedy show, she had just asked one of the bar staff if they could do some comedy, to which he had replied, 'Aw, yeah … I guess, whatever.'

They walked in and the pub was full of assorted people in their late forties dressed in all manner of standard fancy dress costumes. Tommy and Lawrence asked a passing Elvis where the birthday boy was, then proceeded to scan the room for a 50-year-old Harry Potter. After a few minutes they found their man.

'Happy Birthday, Harry!' shouted Lawrence.

'I'm Buddy Holly,' said the bloke. 'That's Harry, the birthday boy, over there.'

After a short conversation, and a few Wingardium Leviosa and Expelliarmus gags, he agreed to let the comedy go ahead. Tommy and Lawrence then headed back to the bar to meet Jenny, first having to fight their way through a group of Teenage Mutant Ninja Turtles and two members of ABBA.

'Where will we be performing?' Tommy asked Jenny, who had somehow successfully reconnoitred the technical details from the vague bar staff.

'Just over there,' she said, pointing to a Morticia on the other side of the room.

'Oh, you mean near the Indiana Jones who is talking to the Captain Jack Sparrow?' asked Tommy.

'No, no,' she said. 'See the guy dressed as Austin Powers?'

'The one next to Wonder Woman, or the one talking to that guy who's either a gangster or an overweight Michael Jackson circa 1982?'

'The one next to Wonder Woman,' said Jenny.

'Yeah, I see him,' said Tommy.

'Just walk up the stairs next to her and there's a space on the balcony for the performance,' said Jenny

'Near Where's Wally?' asked Lawrence.

'No, just next to Batman,' said Jenny.

Tommy was up first and was introduced to a room of crazily dressed people disappointed that the music had stopped and who continued to talk as though loud music was still playing. As he gazed down at the motley collection of superheroes, movie stars and members of the Village People, he noticed that randomly spaced among the crowd were ten people with wet hair, dressed in normal clothes and still holding cheese platters.

One of the most common things that people say when they meet comedians is, 'Tell us a joke,' or, 'Say something funny.' They might as well just say, 'Dance for me, monkey boy!' It is the equivalent of meeting a doctor at a party, pulling down your pants and saying, 'What do you think this rash is?' Or finding out someone works at Officeworks and asking them, 'Why are printer cartridges so fucking expensive?' Actually that's a decent question to ask if you do meet someone from Officeworks. Another annoying thing that people tend to say to comedians is, 'Oh, you're a comedian? I've got a great joke for you that you can use in one of your comedy skits.' Then they launch into the most filthy, distasteful and, usually, racist excuse for a joke you've ever heard and then wait for your reaction. These 'helpful suggestions' for jokes often come from the most unexpected sources in the most unlikely of places.

On the Scaredies' first trip to Edinburgh, we decided to take the scenic route from London and spend a few days driving up to the Scottish capital while experiencing the English countryside. On the second day we stopped overnight at a small bed and breakfast in a quaint little village in the Lake District. Now to simply say that this village was quaint would not be doing justice to its quaintness. If there was a novel entitled *The Quaintest Little Village in All of England* that described how quaintly the quaintness of a quaint village in the realm of Lord Quainty lived out its days in peaceful and picturesque quaintitude, I still don't think that it would accurately capture just how fucking quaint this little village was. It had a very English-sounding name like Carry-on-the-Lake or something like that. Upon arrival, I would not have been surprised to see Winnie the Pooh, Beatrix Potter and Mr Badger strolling arm in arm by the charming stream that trickled under arched stone footbridges surrounded by thatched roof cottages and cobblestone streets. The village was located among a patchwork of small farms that mostly contained quiet groups of sheep or dairy cows. On the outskirts of this tiny village there was a rather large hill, bigger than a hillock yet smaller than a mountain, and the next morning I thought I would get up early and take a walk in the countryside and climb it.

I walked from our accommodation past an inviting-looking pub called the Rose and Crown or the Digglers Inn or something like that, and turned up a tiny lane in the direction of the hill. The lane had no footpath, as the houses and fences were built right up to the edge of the road, so I was forced to walk on the road, which wasn't a bad thing as there was no traffic to speak of, and I certainly wasn't expecting peak hour to begin at any moment. I approached a small dogleg bend in the lane and could hear a strange rumbling sound coming from up ahead, but couldn't see anything because of the corner. As I rounded the bend, I was almost flattened by an enormous flock of sheep that was being herded down the lane by a farmer holding a crook, and his busily barking sheepdog. I stood there stunned, as there was no room to move around them, then I was suddenly grabbed by the shoulder and yanked into a tiny doorway, just as the woolly cavalcade was about to envelop me.

I turned to see who my anonymous rescuer was and saw a diminutive, wiry fellow with enormous grey sideburns that covered half of his face. He had on a well-worn woollen coat and a farmer's hat, and he had a friendly, weather-beaten face with a large pipe hanging out of the side of his mouth. He spoke in a strange accent and said, 'Dat 'twas a close one fer sure, young feller. Wot be ya doin' walkin' op dis here lane?'

'What are you, the feckin cops?' I said. Actually I said, 'I'm just trying to walk up to that big hill over there.'

He looked at me like I was from another planet, and after I told him I was from Australia, I might as well have been.

'Wot ye wanna go op dere for?' he asked, 'Ain't nought but wolves and banshees op dere.'

'Wolves and banshees?'

'Well, ya, moit see a rabbit,' he continued. 'Wot ye doin' here in Carry-on-t'-Lake?'

I told him I was in a comedy group from Australia on our way to perform in Edinburgh. We chatted for a bit more as we waited for the seemingly endless procession of sheep to pass, and I was struck by the lovely, authentic, English countryside experience I was having talking to this rural, dare I say it, quaint bloke in a doorway up a lane in a small country village, when he said, 'Well den, I've got a great joke fer ya, which ye can use in yer act!'

I can't recall what the actual joke was – something to do with a farmer and the inappropriate use of a sheep – let's just say it didn't make it into our set for Edinburgh that year.

So the next time you meet a comedian, don't say, 'Tell us a joke,' or 'Say something funny.' It's annoying, and whatever you do, don't say, 'For a comedian, you don't seem very funny in real life.'

Try asking, 'What's the worst gig you ever played?' That's a much more fun question to answer.

And you ARE ...?

If you spend long enough hanging around in showbiz, it's inevitable, and some would say unfortunate, that eventually you're going to come across some famous people. You might be the support act at their concert, you might be appearing on the same line-up at a festival, or you may cross paths with them when you turn up for a radio or television show. They might ignore you, they might be unaware that you exist, or you might end up having a nice chat in the green room of some theatre or studio or in the backstage tent of an outdoor gig. I would have to say that generally speaking most of the famous people I have met have been nice. Shallow? Sure. Superficial? Probably. Self-obsessed? Highly likely. Of course I've met many people who are not involved in showbiz who were dickheads too, but it takes a special kind of dickhead to make it in showbiz.

I remember the time when I realised that television was a sham. I can't credit that I was once so bright-eyed and innocent as to believe that famous people went on television shows just because they were interesting and had something to offer. I always accepted that it was merely a perfectly timed coincidence that their appearance just happened to coincide with the fact that they had a new show to talk about, or an upcoming tour, or a new album or book or fragrance or fucking pyjamas or whatever useless crap they were desperately trying to peddle to the unsuspecting public. And I only realised it was a sham when I became a part of it.

WHAT, AND GIVE UP SHOWBIZ?

GOOD MORNING AUSTRALIA WITH BERT NEWTON

PAGE 1

DATE: Thursday 6 April 1995 (PRE REC)   EPISODE: 742
(GABN 3/049)

	TIME	NO.	EVENT.	CART	VISION SOURCE.	AUDIO SOURCE.	EST. RUN.
	9.00.27	1	OPENING TITLES	MSO	VTR	SOVTR	.20
		2	BERT OPENING COMMENTS		HOST	N/MIC	1.00
		3	PROMO - ROBERT ENGLUND - JACKI WEAVER - JOHN WATERS - KEN DONE - DR KENNETH COOPER - BRUCE MANSFIELD	003	VTR OLAY		
		4	JOHN FOREMAN		PIANO SET	N/MIC	
		5	BERT INTRO		HOST	N/MIC	
THERESE		6	ROBERT ENGLUND	006	HOST VTR OLAY	N/MIC	8.00
		06A	GRAB: WES CRAVEN'S NEW NIGHTMARE	06A 06B	VTR VTR OLAY SS PICS	SOVTR	( )
		7	BERT THROW TO BREAK		HOST	N/MIC	
		8	BREAKER: Next SCARED WEIRD LITTLE GUYS (SEG: 9.50)	008	VTR/SS	PIANO	
	9.10.17	9	COMM BREAK ONE				3.00

I'm so glad I kept all of this memorabilia. I still can't believe I met Dr Kenneth Cooper

(Rusty Berther)

AND YOU ARE ...?

The first and only time I cracked an invite to the Logies was a bit exciting. If you're wondering how I got to be invited to the Australian television industry's 'night of nights' or, as some would call it, 'night of shite', the Scaredies were actually nominated in the category of 'Best New Talent not from *Home and Away*'. I'm kidding, of course. Everyone knows there is no new talent that is not from *Home and Away*. Why I was really there was because we had been asked to write a funny song about all of the game shows that were featured in that year's television schedule. It was a difficult task, as the brief said we couldn't make fun of Bert Newton or Todd McKenney, and he had just been found passed out in a park, in possession of drugs. Opportunities like that occur very rarely in the topical-songwriting world, so we were behind the eight ball from the start. Nevertheless, we bravely soldiered on, pre-recorded the song, and made our way to a local casino on the date of the invite to enjoy the festivities of the Logies.

John picked me up in a taxi and we exposed our naivety when we arrived at the suggested time of 4.30 pm, which made us, along with the organisers, the wait staff and Richard Wilkins, pretty much the first people to arrive. Our early arrival certainly gave us an unimpeded run down the red carpet, a journey that was as surreal as it was awkward. The crowd was an eclectic mix of overexcited teenagers, *TV Week* readers and members of what I can only imagine is called the Loud Screamers Club, three non-mutually exclusive groups. They stood five deep either side of a winding, fenced carpet that led from where the cars drop the guests off to the escalators about 100 metres away. At the halfway point of the red carpet journey, the pathway opens out to a more spacious area for photo opportunities and 'interviews'. John and I strolled through that section without causing too much trouble to anybody, and a few photographers graciously tested out their flashes on us, to make us feel included. There were a few well-wishers in the crowd, some even called us over to sign things, and I was more than happy to scrawl 'All the best, Peter Helliar' on whatever was held in front of me.

Feeling a little chuffed that some people had actually recognised me, I was quickly brought back to earth when we reached the check-in table.

'Name please?' asked the prim-looking girl behind the desk.

'Rusty Berther,' I replied, as she began searching for my name on the list. 'Sorry, that name is not here,' she said, as she simultaneously tilted her head and shrunk her mouth into the shape of a cat's bum. I looked down at the name cards that were arranged in alphabetical order on the table and saw a name card that said 'Rusty Berner'.

'Ah, I think that's mine right there,' I said, pointing to the card.

'Do you have any ID?' said cat's bum girl

'I have ID for Rusty *Berther*,' I said to her, 'But the name on that card is obviously incorrect. There is no one called Rusty Berner out there.'

'Well, I've seen his show,' she said smugly.

'You're thinking of *Peter* Berner,' I said, wishing I had a vial of acid to throw in her face. 'He's about a foot taller than I am, he's bald, wears glasses and has a goatee.'

'I think I know what Rusty Berner looks like,' she spat.

'Rusty!' said another woman, approaching the table. 'Is there a problem?'

'Yes, this girl doesn't know her ABC television presenters from her unknown musical comedy performers,' I said angrily.

I was saved by the nice lady from the Channel Nine publicity department and had finally gained entry to the fabled foyer bar of the Logies. As we walked in the entrance, we were greeted by two long lines of drink waiters standing in formation and holding trays filled with colourful drinks. It was like a guard of honour for alcoholics. I didn't want to be rude, so I grabbed a drink from each of the first four trays I passed, then realised that it was the Logies and there was probably about 11 hours of drinking to go and I had to pace myself, so I wisely put one of the drinks back.

I have never been in a room that involved so many conversations with people constantly looking over your shoulder to see who else they could be talking to. It's not just your shoulder they look over, either. Your shoulder, their shoulder, the shoulders of any person walking past, they're not fussy. Talk about being given the cold shoulder. Ironically it was enough to give me a chip on mine and I felt like I needed one to cry on, but I recovered quickly as another tray of drinks whizzed past.

Many people that are in the room at the Logies are recognisable, plus with the Scaredies having worked around the traps for so many years, I had met or worked with many of them in some capacity. That combined with a few champagnes made it difficult to work out if I knew someone or had just seen them on the telly. That didn't stop me nodding a smiley 'hello' to many people, some of whom simply stared back at me with a look of bewildered indifference before returning their own smiley 'hello'.

I saw the bald guy from Hi-5 looking at me, and we simultaneously realised that we recognised each other, without knowing one another. Bit weird.

After an hour or so of mingling around the bar outside the main ballroom, it was time for everyone to take their seats for the next seven hours of entertainment.

Trying to get the Logies crowd away from the bar and seated at their tables is like having sex with Madonna: it takes a long time, there's a lot of complaining and at some stage, Molly Meldrum is going to get upset.

Upon threat of missing out on our entrée, John and I joined the masses and moved into the glamorous main room. With our song already recorded, we had no lyrics to memorise or performance to stress about, so we merely had to sit back and enjoy the night, and by 'sit back' I mean sit *at* the back and enjoy the night, as our table was situated so far away from the action that the sound desk was closer to the stage than we were. We shared a table with some folks on about the same level as us in the pecking order of the Australian television industry – relatives of a Channel Nine executive and some *TV Week* competition winners – and passed the evening by betting on who would win each category. Usually that would keep the night interesting but even that wore thin after a while. I couldn't help thinking there must be some crazy idea for a television show that I could come up with to give some of the shows a run for their money.

After a few more hours we played a game which involved counting how many *Home and Away* cast members you could physically bump into and apologise to while on a trip to the toilets. We watched some of the overseas stars strut their stuff on the stage, then around this point in the evening details become a little sketchy. Trying to recall the events of the rest of the night is a bit like when Harry Potter uses Dumbledore's pensieve to retrieve past memories. My vision of the night becomes a swirling, shimmering mass of faces and people who don't respond to me when I talk to them.

Here are some memories that are either parts of my night from the rest of the Logies, or things that I dreamed later on:

I spoke to Brisbane Lions player and ex-coach Michael Voss in a self-conscious five-minute conversation about AFL and what the hell he was doing there.

I talked to, with or at Garry Lyon from *The Footy Show* for a while. Good old Garry didn't look over my shoulder for someone else to talk to. He didn't have to. His height meant he could simply look over my head to an unimpeded smorgasbord of potential new conversations. I think he lost interest around the point when I started a sentence, 'You know whatsh wrong with footy these days …'

I went up to a Channel Ten female newsreader and said, 'I know your brother,' because one of the boys from the comedy group Elbow Skin had once told me that he was this particular newsreader's brother, and I had always remembered it whenever I had seen her on the telly. She said to me, 'I don't have a brother.' Then she walked away. I consoled myself with the fact that at least she hadn't looked over my shoulder to see who else she could talk too, though as the entire conversation lasted about 2.3 seconds, she didn't really have time.

I guess the night ended without any major embarrassment, because I checked the papers the next day and, funnily enough, there was no mention of me at all. I caught a taxi home and remember speaking to the African driver about his life in refugee camps, sending money home to his family and eventually bringing them out to their new home in Australia. I thought, 'Now there's a "home and away" story that puts the whole thing into perspective.'

I've never met any big-name Hollywood actors, but the Phones, my old a cappella group, once sang to seven people at a dinner party at a film producer's house in Toorak. That sounds like a small audience, but to be fair there had originally been eight guests but one of them had felt a bit sick and gone home early. It was an aspiring young actor you may have heard of, named Robert De Niro. I don't know what caused him to miss our performance.

Possibly the prawn cocktail had not agreed with him, or maybe he just wasn't a fan of a cappella music. I'm blaming the prawn cocktail.

At a hotel in Montreal I once shared a lift with the actor David Schwimmer. We chatted for ages about all kinds of stuff, starting with him asking, 'Could you hold the door, please?' as he rushed to catch the lift. That was about it, really. During the awkward 15 seconds of lift silence that followed, where you find yourself standing next to another human and both of you know you will never see the other person ever again, I did the standard smile with pursed lips accompanied by a slight nod of the head that is universally acknowledged as saying, '*Hello, I am a not a weirdo, and I have no desire to make small talk with you, as there is nothing that will be accomplished conversationally by asking you any sort of question, as I can see by the lift button you pressed that we will only have a short time together. Nonetheless, I wish you and your family all the best in whatever you do in the future.*' Then the lift doors opened and we went our separate ways.

So that's it for me in the Hollywood star stakes, though there was that time I met Meryl Streep; I guess that counts. After those dubious stories about Robert De Niro and David Schwimmer, you're probably thinking, 'Oh, sure you met Meryl Streep. What, you watched one of her movies one time? Or you saw her at Dreamworld when she was brought out by KFC for the *Big Brother* finale?'

I can't believe you think that I would say that I met Meryl Streep just so I could mention it here. Okay, I admit that *met* Meryl Streep might not be entirely accurate. For the record, I sat next to her on the set of the movie *Evil Angels* and our arms touched. That was it, but it was just after we acted together in the same scene.

It was in the late 1980s, and my fabricated acting resumé

had obviously done the trick, because I had somehow scored a full week of extra work on *Evil Angels*. Each day I would drive in my clapped-out blue Volkswagen beetle to an outer suburb of Melbourne where the night-time Ayers Rock campground scenes were being filmed inside an enormous, blacked-out industrial shed. I played the role of 'onlooker holding a torch' (unfortunately uncredited) during the scene where the dingo had just taken the baby. Fifteen minutes into the film, if you pause the video at the correct place (I'm not sure if it has been released on DVD yet), I can be seen wearing a blue checked jacket in the background between Sam Neill and Meryl Streep. I am looking slightly blurred due to the fact I was standing about 50 metres away from the action, though if the camera had zoomed in you would have easily made out the appallingly over-acted look on my face that said, 'Ooh-what's-going-on-over-there-I-was-just-sitting-here-camping-when-I-heard-a-scream-so-I-grabbed-my-torch-and-came-as-fast-as-I-could!'

That one scene was pretty much the five days of extra work for me, though there were a few long shots of all of the extras walking around in the dark with torches. It was a fun experience for someone like me who had no aspirations to go any further in the movie industry, to see some famous stars. Though we were given strict instructions never to talk to Meryl Streep while we were around the set. Most of the five days of 'work' was spent hanging around outside the giant shed in a large marquee with the 50 or so other extras, playing cards, reading, eating and overhearing wankers talk about their 'acting' careers.

At one point on the fourth day I was in the middle of a rather cracking game of five hundred with three other extras, when a wardrobe lady came rushing out of the shed and into the extras' holding pen. She quickly analysed the faces of me and the three chaps I was playing cards with then said to me, 'Stand up.'

I stood up.

'What size are you?' she asked.

'Thirty-two,' I replied, hoping she was referring to my pants.

She grabbed my arm and said 'Come with me.'

I was unsure whether I was being taken to do some acting, or to be the next disposable toy boy for some big shot Hollywood producer.

Thankfully it was for some extra work. I was ushered swiftly and silently into the darkened shed and made to change into the uniform of a Northern Territory park ranger. Finally someone had recognised my obvious talent and chosen me to play the vital role of Park Ranger # 4.

I was taken onto the set and told to sit silently in a chair. It was one of those classic director's chairs, and mine had the name 'Sam Neill' on the back of it. The chair next to me had 'Meryl Streep' on it, but she was nowhere to be seen. Neither was Sam Neill, which explained why I got to sit in his chair. I then got to spend a most interesting few hours watching the workings of a major movie set. They were filming a couple of scenes that took place immediately after the disappearance of Azaria Chamberlain, and Meryl Streep, playing Lindy Chamberlain, had to maintain the constant unfortunate state of someone whose baby had just been stolen and eaten by a dingo. She spent most of the time between takes sitting by herself and being sad in the small tent that was playing the coveted role of the 'Chamberlains' tent'. Watching her being continually upset gave me a small insight into just how difficult that must be to do, because it certainly didn't look like much fun.

Occasionally she would come over and sit in the chair next to me. She would stare straight ahead or check her script, and I was too frightened to even look at her, let alone say anything. At one point she dropped her pencil and as she bent down to pick it up

AND YOU ARE ...?

```
RESUME  FOR RUSSELL BERTHER -Musician,Actor

Address:-    3/124 Inkerman st. St. Kilda
Phone:-      5347822
Age:--       19
Details:-    6 years experience singing,playing,performing.
      :-     proficient on a number of instruments;guitar
             bass guitar,mandolin,banjelele.
      :-     performed for two years in comedy/cabaret band
             in Brisbane 85/86; toured Sydney mid 85; appeared
             on locally released video made by Channel 9.
      :-     toured Central Qld. with the Kelvin Grove Big
             Band '84
      :-     played in Radio 4BK Christmas Spectacular '85.
      :-     member of winning vocal group S.E.Q.S.A. champ-
             ion ships '84.
      :-     worked as extra on Holiday Island '83.
      :-     done session singing on various television jingles
             '85/'86.
      :-     sang and played in hotels around Brisbane '86.
      :-     performed and played in amateur plays and musicals
             since 1982.
```

My hand-typed resumé that I used to join Actors Equity so I could meet Meryl Streep. Some of it is true
(Rusty Berther)

our elbows rubbed, thereby giving me, for the rest of my life, the chance to say that I have literally rubbed elbows with Meryl Streep. I thought about giving her a quick, pursed-lip, '*I'm not a weirdo ... etc.*' smile with a nod of the head, but chose not to because, you know, it might have thrown her off her character and that. After a few hours of being ignored by everyone, including the girl who offered to make everybody a cup of tea, I was released from the set. I guess they were content to just have the three park rangers, and I would have merely complicated things too much.

WHAT, AND GIVE UP SHOWBIZ?

Harry Doupe is a stand-up comedian from Vancouver, Canada, with whom the Scaredies shared the bill with for a gig in Northern Ontario in the mid-1990s. On the long drive to the show, the conversation was flowing from topic to topic, as it does on these sorts of long drives, and after a while the chat drifted on to music and important issues such as Australian bands versus Canadian bands. We were having a heated discussion concerning the respective musical merits of Men at Work versus Loverboy, and much as I'm loathe to admit it, Loverboy was winning. As we were going to have to listen to the winning Canadian band's album, I can at least thank God that Nickelback hadn't been invented yet.

With that settled, we moved on to another burning question: who is more Australian – Kylie Minogue or AC/DC? At first you might think it's obvious, but it's more difficult than you think when you start comparing some of the similarities between these two unlikely artists:

Neither has lived in Australia for many years.

Both have a long list of hit singles and have achieved success in Australia and internationally.

And thirdly, except for Kylie, both have a lead singer that died choking on his own vomit.

So when you look at it like that, it's difficult to tell who is more Australian. Hence the valuable discussion that was entertaining us all on the long drive.

Then Harry said, 'I've got Bon Scott's cap.'

'What, like you've got a cap that's similar to one Bon Scott used to wear?' I asked.

'No,' he said, 'I've got Bon Scott's actual cap that he used to wear. He gave it to me.'

Well then, I thought, we've still got two hours of the drive to go, so let's hear the story.

Harry took us back to late 1977, just outside Vancouver, BC. He and his two best mates, Chris and Brad, were in their mid-teens and avid music junkies. They had an ongoing contest to see who could be the first to discover the next band that they couldn't live without. Their level of competitiveness meant that they would often buy albums by bands they had never heard of, just based on album covers that looked like they held something loud, cool and aggressive within. Many a time that spelled dissatisfaction or outright anger, certainly a feeling of failure if the band didn't meet their musical expectations.

One day in late 1977, Brad showed up at Harry's house with an album he had found. It had a cover that left little doubt that inside was something belligerent, maybe a little dangerous, and certainly very LOUD. Any of them would have bought it, but Brad had the distinction of discovering it first. It was an album by an unknown band called AC/DC, titled *Let There Be Rock*. Even if you only saw the back cover, you would have been sold – titles such as 'Dog Eat Dog', 'Let There Be Rock', 'Bad Boy Boogie' and 'Problem Child' basically ended the contest before the needle hit the vinyl. The guitar sound was so big! They were all sold immediately and spent the next months trying to convert any of their friends that would listen to AC/DC, along with another new band they'd found, called Van Halen.

Cut to the next spring. AC/DC had released a new album called *Powerage* and this one sounded even louder. Right around this time, an ad appeared in the *Vancouver Sun*'s entertainment section, announcing the first local appearance in years of Aerosmith, and at first the cartoon drawing of the band used in the ad took attention away from the small lettering underneath:

'With Special Guests – AC/DC'

Harry didn't even bother to call his mates. He jumped in his beat-up 1964 Ford Falcon, newspaper on the front seat beside him, *Powerage* blasting through the tinny speakers, and drove straight to Chris's house. They couldn't believe it. AC/DC were coming to town!

It should be mentioned that Harry was a keen collector of autographs and he had got pretty good at tracking down touring artists. One trick he'd learned was that if he called some of the main city hotels the day before a band was supposed to be there, often the reservations would be under their real names, and then the names were changed once they checked in. He would just ask to speak to the room of someone from the band, the receptionist would spend some time looking up the reservation and then usually say there was nobody under that name listed. Then Harry would simply say, 'Maybe I had the date wrong, can you check tomorrow?' It was a rarity, but sometimes they would come back on the phone and say that yes, the band were scheduled at the hotel, but not until the next day. Then Harry would go and camp out by the hotel and wait for the touring band to arrive. One of the hotels he tried that day was the Vancouver Holiday Inn.

'Holiday Inn City Centre, how may I direct your call?'

'Yeah, can you give me Bon Scott's room?' said Harry in a lowered voice, trying to sound important.

'Just a moment – I'll check for that listing,' said the woman on the other end of the phone.

Almost immediately Harry heard the phone click and then ring and a raspy voice answered. Back in those pre-internet days, touring information was next to impossible to come by. Something that had never even occurred to Harry had happened. The band had a day off, and had already arrived in Vancouver before their show on the following night.

'Hello?' said the raspy voice.

AND YOU ARE ...?

'Is this Bon?'

'Yeah, who's this?'

More than a little frazzled, Harry said, 'Uh, my name's Harry and we're big fans of the band and wondered if we could come in and get something autographed?'

Bon replied in the positive and asked if Harry was in the lobby. Harry said he could be there in about an hour.

Bon said, 'No worries, just call me when you get here.'

Harry hung up the phone and called Chris and Brad, trying not to freak out. He told them to get ready, they were going to meet AC/DC. Ten minutes later the three of them were in Harry's car driving to the Vancouver Holiday Inn. They were all Thunderstruck, thinking, 'Hells Bells, we're gonna Ride On the Highway to Hell to meet a Rock 'n' Roll Singer.'

Those puns are my own addition to Harry's story, and half of them are not even songs that feature Bon Scott, so, ahem, back to Harry and the boys.

They arrived at the lobby of the hotel and got reception to call Bon's room. Before they knew it, they were negotiating the confusing hallways and knocking on a door that swung open to reveal none other than Bon fucking Scott, in all his dishevelled glory.

He was dressed in his customary tight jeans and t-shirt, and on his head he wore a black Greek fisherman's cap. He was instantly friendly and asked the boys to come in and sit down and proceeded to ask them all about themselves and their musical tastes. All Harry had to get signed was the newspaper ad for the concert and a picture he had cut out of some rock magazine. What was immediately clear was that Bon wasn't in any hurry to get rid of them, which was surprising and awesome, and he began to call up the other guys in the band to get them to come over and autograph Harry's soon-to-be-prized newspaper clipping.

Being his first trip to Canada, Bon asked the boys a load of questions about their home, how many people lived there, how long it took to travel across the country, things like that, and while those discussions were happening, Malcolm Young and Cliff Williams stopped in separately to sign autographs and say hello. At a certain point Bon asked them about the drug laws in Canada, and how severe they might be. Chris said that the laws weren't tough at all and Bon asked them if by any chance they knew where he might be able to purchase something illegal and smokeable. While none of the boys were pot smokers, they knew a guy. Now, this being Vancouver in the 1970s, buying and selling marijuana was a great deal more underground than it currently is; nowadays it's about as tough as spotting a mountain or breathing air. So Harry used Bon's hotel phone to call their friend, who didn't believe them when they told him Bon Scott of AC/DC wanted to buy some pot. But he came around when he was invited to come with them to meet Bon. The boys left the hotel and made it out to their pot supplying friend and were back in about an hour and a half. By this time it was early evening and Bon had finished a room service meal and a bottle or two of Blue Nun white wine. Also in the room with Bon was AC/DC's drummer, Phil Rudd, who was planning to go and see jazz legend Buddy Rich that night at the Cave Nightclub. Harry got Phil to sign his paper and, as he had earlier run into Angus Young in the hotel lobby, he now had all of the bandmembers' signatures.

Now into the herb, and having ordered a couple more bottles of wine, Bon was just this great guy having a good time hanging out with some fans, and Harry and his mates were as happy as could be. Harry asked about the tour, and Bon jumped up from his chair and began to rifle through his suitcase. He pulled out a black t-shirt and asked if Harry wanted it. It was from the show they had played the day before, and of course Harry took the gift.

AND YOU ARE ...?

The front of the shirt had a green, yellow and white event logo, and the back was evidence of just how unknown AC/DC really was at that time. It read:

Bill Graham Presents
A Day On The Green

And in descending order from the headliners down:

Aerosmith
Foreigner
Pat Travers
Van Halen
AC/DC
Oakland Coliseum
July 23, 1978

Hindsight being what it is, especially after 35 years, that running order looks insane. I mean, sure, we all like Pat Travers, but c'mon, ahead of Van Halen *and* AC/DC? But back then that's exactly who AC/DC were: unknowns on their first North American tour, still a year or more away from breaking through.

Harry and his mates really didn't want the night to end, but they didn't want to overstay their welcome either, so after a couple more bottles of Blue Nun, with everyone in good spirits, the boys decided to head home. As they were leaving the room, Harry said to Bon, 'Hey Bon, I like your cap.'

Bon took the cap off and replied, 'Well, if you like it so much, you can have it,' and handed the cap to Harry.

Picture the thrill of a young music fan who has just spent the night chatting away to the legendary Bon Scott from AC/DC. And not just chatting like some fair-weather fan, Harry had actually connected with, and obviously made such an impression on Bon that he was now the owner of a precious piece of rock history. This cap was a thing to be closely treasured. It had Bon's sweat on it. It had some of Bon's hair in it. This cap smelled like Bon Scott … actually maybe it wasn't a thing to be treasured too closely.

The next night Harry and the boys went to the concert and AC/DC were fantastic, capped off by Angus travelling through the crowd on Bon's shoulders and winning over a Pacific Coliseum crowd that had no idea, for the most part, who this Australian band was.

Harry's favourite part of the night, however, was before the show. They had camped out by the back doors of the Coliseum and wanted to say hi to Bon and the rest of AC/DC when they all arrived. After all, they were practically best friends with the band now.

Harry was, of course, wearing his new Bon Scott cap and was standing with his friends as the AC/DC tour bus pulled up. He couldn't wait to see the look on Bon's face when he recognised him and his cap from the night before. Bon Scott stepped off the bus and Harry said, 'Hey, Bon!'

Bon looked directly at Harry and said, 'Hey, nice cap, I've got one just like it!'

Did I ever tell you about the time that I weed in Adam Hills' car? It's okay – Adam was in the car at the time, and he knew that I was in the car – he just didn't know that I did some wee in his car. He still doesn't, as far as I'm aware. Sure, he may have got in his car on the next hot day and thought to himself, 'That's weird, I don't remember a tom cat spraying on my passenger seat.'

So I am pretty sure he is still unaware of what was going on at the time. Of course I *think* he didn't know what I was up to in that way that drunk people think they are acting quite normally in front of a sober person but the sober person is thinking, 'Why is this drunk person acting so weirdly and trying to act sober?'

By the way, it wasn't a full-blown empty-the-bladder type of a wee in Adam's car, just a couple of drops ... I think.

It was after the final-ever recording of the television show *Spicks and Specks*. The ABC had pulled out all stops to put on a lavish party in the Gordon Street studio's cafeteria. Of course it would be a cheap shot to do a joke about how the ABC has no money, and that they had to throw the party in the studio cafeteria, but it was not like that at all. It was obvious they had made a special effort to say goodbye to the show, as there were some streamers covering up the fluorescent lights around the cafeteria menu board and I counted at least seven balloons. Nonetheless, it was a pretty good party. There was a seemingly endless stream of trays laden with a stunning array of delicious hors d'oeuvres, some of which were not deep-fried.

Playing in one corner of the cafeteria was a band that featured ex-stars of 1980s bands. They were called 'Men Without Hair' or 'Beer Gut 100' or something like that, and they were quite entertaining. It was an honour to be invited to such a prestigious and exclusive event, and there was a small crowd of about 600 people crammed into a room that would usually comfortably fit about 40.

I spent the night chatting to various other freeloaders and past guests from the show, and before I knew it, it was late, the show and speeches had finished and the room had thinned out considerably. It was around about that time when I realised that I was drunk, I needed to go home, I needed to pee and I had had enough fun – but not in that order. I was on my way to the men's toilets when I was distracted by a group of people causing a commotion. It was the type of commotion that you would only ever witness at a television station party involving alcohol and freeloaders like myself. A generous production assistant was handing out cab charges to a crowd of eager inebriates, so I enthusiastically joined the throng, grabbed a couple and then proceeded to try and scab a lift home with someone. At this point, Adam overheard me and very graciously offered me a lift home, as we both live in the same suburb.

'Hey, Rusty,' he offered 'I'll give you a lift, but I am leaving right now.'

'Oh great,' I thought, 'a lift with conditions.'

'Are you coming or what?' he said

'Okay, how about losing the attitude, peg leg!' I snapped back. I didn't really say that last bit and Adam was more than happy to drop me off on his way home. Understandably, it had been a huge night for him and he would have been exhausted, though he was still annoyingly cheerful and completely sober.

As we started walking out the door to leave, I realised I still had to pee, but I didn't want to hold up Adam any longer, so I kept walking. His car was parked over at the *Spicks and Specks* offices, which were a five-minute walk away.

Now I know Adam reasonably well – he has sung songs with the Scaredies Superband half a dozen times, I have been on his TV shows a bit and we have run into each other at festivals around the world and had a chat, but we have never really hung out together and are not *that* familiar with each other. So I didn't really feel comfortable just having a quick wizz by a tree on someone's nature strip in front of him.

I should have.

We were chatting away as we got into his car. Sitting down was not comfortable, as it just added pressure to my bursting bladder. I mentally pictured the journey home and thought, 'I can do this,

I can do this ... I *have* to do this! It'll just be 15 minutes tops at this time of night with no traffic, I can make it!' Then we started driving over a series of 12 speed bumps, which added to the agony and made my voice waver as we drove over each bump.

I thought, 'Uh oh, was that a little drop?' as we cleared the final speed bump. I dared not look down, and tried to concentrate on the conversation to keep me distracted. We were having a nice chat about my recent marathon in Antarctica and what I had been up to since the Scaredies had finished and what Adam was going to do now that *Spicks* had ended. In my mind I was doing quite well, asking all the right questions, with just the occasional slight slurring of words. I was aware that Adam had not had a drink, and I was feeling a little self-conscious. I didn't want to be the slurry drunk guy getting a lift home with the host of a successful show that had just shot its final episode. We've all been there before, right? Anyway, I was over-compensating by trying to use bigger words than I normally would.

'So, you're going to the UK to host a new TV show ... how meritorious ...'

But it came out like, 'How meritorioushh.'

Five minutes into the drive and I seriously doubted if I was going to make it home without unleashing two or three litres of kidney-filtered beer onto the floor of Adam's car.

I couldn't talk any more. Whenever Adam said something, I crossed my legs awkwardly, nodded and made a high-pitched 'hmm' sound while exhaling loudly through my nose.

God, was that another drip? It was difficult to tell, as there was a general feeling of numbness growing around my lower abdominal area, like I had had an epidural and was preparing for childbirth. My body was going into some kind of survival mode as it sensed I was drowning from the inside. I was shifting from cheek to cheek, uncrossing and crossing my arms and

WHAT, AND GIVE UP **SHOWBIZ?**

Hey, Adam, whatever you do, don't drink what's in that glass
(Rich Hardcastle)

desperately trying not to think about anything related to water, hoses or plumbing in general.

At one point I said, 'Just let me out here, this will be fine.'

'But we're on the Westgate Bridge,' said Adam.

After the bridge I knew there were only three sets of traffic lights to go. I was digging deep and using mental powers of self-control that would have put Uri Geller to shame.

Finally we approached the end of my street and I said with fake politeness through clenched teeth, 'Here we are, just on the corner is fine.'

Adam responded graciously, 'Really, I can take you right to yo–'

'I said here is fine!' I shouted, tears forming in my eyes.

'Okay-thanks-for-the-lift-Adam-see-you-soon,' I quickly mumbled, opened the door and got out as the car was still moving. I was out of the car and as far as I knew he was still none the wiser. I had made it and as Adam's car disappeared around the corner, I fumbled with my pants and got on with the business of relieving myself.

Oh what sweet, sweet relief.

I don't know how long I stood there watering a neighbour's nature strip, it may have been two minutes, it may have been ten. I was about halfway through and thinking that even if the cops drove by and pulled guns on me, I wouldn't have been able to stop. A car suddenly pulled around the corner and screeched to a halt. The window rolled down, it was Adam looking for directions back to his house.

'Oh, did you need to pee?' he said, 'You should have said something and I would have stopped!'

There was one quite noisy, talkative audience that the Scaredies played to at a corporate gig, where we encountered the most unlikely of saviours.

This particular gig was a $250-a-head, gala fundraiser for a hospital, and there were about 1200 well-to-do folks in attendance who were plied with a sumptuous three-course meal and lashings of booze so that the organisers could fleece some big donations for their very worthy cause.

There was a steady stream of big name entertainers and bands booked for the night, and the venue was the Palladium ballroom at the prestigious Crown Casino in Melbourne, home to both the Logies and the Brownlow. Actually not that prestigious, really. We felt very special and well looked after when we were shown to our dressing room and started helping ourselves to the rather large, immaculately arranged plate of gourmet sandwiches and cheese platter that had been generously supplied. I felt a little bit suspicious after downing my fifth smoked salmon and asparagus sanger with the crusts cut off, when I noticed there was also a lavish drinks rider, containing a couple of slabs of beer on ice, a dozen bottles of wine, a bottle of single malt whiskey and two bottles of Stolichnaya vodka. That's when I realised we had accidentally been shown to Jimmy Barnes' dressing room. We panicked and quickly rearranged the sandwiches, grabbed a bottle of vodka and got the hell out of there. Our real dressing room was actually just down the hallway in the much larger green room that we were sharing with the swing band. They were nice blokes and more of our style anyway, plus they kept a look out while I returned for Barnesy's cheese platter, which we all shared.

When it was our turn to perform, the night had been underway for over three hours and the crowd was very talkative and half tanked. We were on after the auction, which, for a comedy act, is the worst possible thing to follow. You might as well just shout at the audience unintelligibly for 20 minutes and then say, 'Now here's some comedy.'

The emcee, John Blackman, finally announced that the last item up for auction was a brand new motorcycle that had a very fast sounding name like the Kwakajima QX-78000, and it was to be ridden into the Palladium by a special guest Hollywood movie star. I could sense everyone in the room trying to work out what second-rate Hollywood star had been a guest on that Channel Ten info/news/comedy/lifestyle/panel show that week, *The 6 pm Promo*, or whatever it's called these days. But before anyone had time to speculate whether the star driver was John Travolta or one of the knuckleheads from Good Charlotte, the sound of a loud engine revving was heard which quickly became the very loud sound of a motorcycle been ridden into the ballroom for a few laps of the dance floor. The driver eventually stopped, got off the bike and took his helmet off. Everyone in the room gasped. Not because they recognised the rider, but because the exhaust fumes from the motorcycle had made it virtually impossible to breathe. Then there was a bit of stunned silence, followed by the incoherent mumbling of half of the room going, 'Who is? ... I dunno ... Do you know? ... Is that Alan Brough?'

Thankfully, we were all saved by John Blackman announcing, 'Ladies and Gentlemen would you please put your hands together for Mr Peter Fonda!'

There was a bit more, 'Who? ... Do you know? ... What's he from...?'

'The star of *Easy Rider*,' continued John Blackman.

Finally there was some applause and a bit of recognition as the crowd started to realise, 'Oh yeah, the father of Bridget Fonda and surely somehow related to Jane Fonda.'

There he was all right. Peter Fonda was in Melbourne making a film and somehow he had been roped in to help auction off a

Japanese motorcycle at a charity function. He walked from where he had parked the motorcycle on the dance floor, up the stairs and onto the stage where he participated in a somewhat bewildering interview with John Blackman for about 20 minutes.

He was a little incoherent – but then he does have a history of LSD use going back about 50 years, so he wasn't doing too badly. It wasn't that his accent was hard to understand either; just that sometimes it was difficult to comprehend what language he was speaking. I don't know what he had been imbibing, but I am positive that by riding that motorcycle he was breaking at least three separate driving under the influence laws.

When Mr Fonda's interview was finished, he made his way back down on to the dance floor while the motorcycle was auctioned (it went for over $100,000) and enthusiastically greeted the new owner, who, I must say, looked a little stunned at the fact that he had just paid that much money for a motorbike.

With all that out of the way, the Scaredies were finally introduced to a smattering of applause that was well drowned out by the crowd, at least half of whom were now out of their seats and wandering among the tables chatting.

Our set was only 20 minutes long and we had been in similar situations before, so we have pretty thick skins when it comes to circumstances like that. The sound was good and we could hear ourselves clearly so it was a case of steamroll ahead and get through the set then get the hell offstage. We were halfway through our second song – the Australian Tourism deadly animals song – when I noticed that Peter Fonda had been watching us from the dance floor and he was now walking towards the stage.

'Oh no,' I thought, 'he isn't, is he?'

He continued walking up the stairs.

'He's not going to – he wouldn't, would he?'

He was walking straight towards us.

'Yep, he is. He's going to gra–'

Peter Fonda grabbed the microphone from my hand, I was in the middle of singing a line of the song, but he was oblivious. He stood in between John and myself with his arm around my shoulders.

'People!' he shouted distortedly, half into the microphone and half into my face. I caught a whiff of his breath and my knees slightly buckled.

'People! Listen up!' he continued loudly, 'These here are my boys!'

I swear we never met the guy before.

'You gotta give these boys a go!' he shouted.

There was about a five per cent reduction in the overall noise level, though a few more people started taking notice.

'Come on folks!' he shouted into my face and I believe I may have momentarily lost consciousness.

'Let's keep it down for these guys!'

He turned and handed the mike back to me and said, 'There you go, fellas.'

'Er ... thanks.'

The microphone reeked of a mixture of whiskey, cigarette smoke and Tic Tacs so I swapped it with the one on John's stand, as his both his hands were busy playing the guitar.

Peter Fonda wandered back down the stairs and spent the remainder of our set watching from in front of the stage, dancing to some of the jokes.

Lano and Woodley were hosting *Hey Hey It's Saturday*. They were dressed in their usual gear – Colin in a suit and Frank wearing his old fisherman's hat.

```
                HEY HEY IT'S SATURDAY
                   REHEARSAL ORDER

                                          LIVE
                                          TX:SAT 26TH NOV, 1994
                                          HHIS/94-042


   2:00     TORI AMOS                     LIVE VOCAL/BT/PIANO
            "CORNFLAKE GIRL"               CENTRE


   2:30     BAND CALL - TOMMY EMMANUEL    BANDSET
            "STEVIE'S BLUES"


   3:00     SCARED WEIRD LITTLE GUYS


   3:30     BOYZ II MEN                   4 LIVE VOCAL/BT
            "ON BENDED KNEE"              CENTRE


   4:15     KYLIE MINOGUE                 LIVE VOCAL/BT
            "PUT YOURSELF IN MY PLACE"    CENTRE
            "CONFIDE IN ME" (4 STRINGS/PERC)


   5:15     RECORD PROMO


   6:15     CHECK CROSSES
```

We did around 20 spots on *Hey Hey It's Saturday* and this was a typical lineup. I remember 'meeting' Kylie as she sat in a makeup chair near me, though I imagine she doesn't remember meeting me

(Rusty Berther)

One of the guests was Barry Manilow who came on the set with the face of a 40 year old and the hair of a Siberian husky. I don't know if his hair was real but it certainly wasn't his.

He was introduced by Frank and Col and took the applause and said to Frank, 'Hey, I like your hat.'

Quick as a flash Frank replied, 'Hey, I like yours too.'
Well played, Frank, well played.

David and Shane, the Umbilical Brothers, were performing for the first time in Los Angeles in a tiny 50-seat theatre. They had received some rave reviews for their off-Broadway show entitled *Thwack!*, that they had been performing for the previous six months in New York City. They had scored a couple of television spots on the Jay Leno show and were now giving the LA theatre scene a try. With the theatre being so small, they could see the audience members quite clearly, and one night David was stunned to look out into the audience of about 15 people and see Eric Idle of Monty Python sitting there, right next to Billy Connolly. That made for a nervous performance and the boys were quite chuffed after the show, despite the small crowd. The next night Billy Connolly's wife Pamela Stephenson came along with a couple of their children, obviously on a recommendation from Billy. She stayed around after the show to introduce herself and the kids, taking the opportunity to say hello to some fellow Australians. When David mentioned that they had seen Billy and Eric in the audience the night before, Pamela said, 'Yes, they really loved the show and waited for you both for quite a while.'

'Waited for us where?' asked Shane.

Pamela said, 'Oh, Eric and Billy were waiting for you in the restaurant across the street after the show. They wanted to buy you dinner, but you mustn't have got the message.'

Mustn't have got the message! Of all the messages that you could not have passed on to you, why couldn't it have been, 'Your dental appointment is confirmed for tomorrow,' and not the one that says, 'Billy Connolly and Eric Idle are waiting to buy you dinner at the restaurant across the street'!

Australian actor Frank Thring was a flamboyant, theatrical figure best known for his role as Pontius Pilate in the movie *Ben Hur*. He has been described by those who knew him as eccentric, intimidating and often cruelly sarcastic, with a dry wit and a very distinctive voice.

In the early 1990s, Frank had recorded a very amusing voice-over promo for Melbourne community radio station 3RRR's annual radiothon. Over the next few months, the promo proved so popular with the listeners that Frank was called back to record more voice-overs. Triple R employee Malcolm Scott was in charge of recording all of the station promos, so he was the one who dealt with Frank Thring whenever he came in. Malcolm got to know Frank quite well, and would even drop by for a cup of tea at Frank's house, which was just around the corner from the 3RRR studios.

Frank was booked to record another voice-over at ten o'clock one Monday morning, and Malcolm had arrived early, as Frank was always reliably on time. Ten-thirty came and went and Malcolm called Frank's house, but no one answered. After 11 am Malcolm was getting a little concerned, so he decided to walk around the corner to Frank's house, thinking he had possibly overslept. Malcolm knocked a few times and, though no one answered, he thought he could hear movement inside the house. Thinking Frank might be in trouble, Malcolm went around to the rear of the house and peered in through the glass doors. He was not prepared for the sight that greeted him. Frank was tied to a chair, wearing nothing but a pair of black underpants, his arms and feet were bound and he had a large piece of black gaffer tape across his mouth. Malcolm broke in, worried that Frank was in trouble. He tore the tape from Frank's mouth and Frank simply said, 'What a fabulous weekend!'

Another Frank Thring story involves Frank's performance in a play called *The Kingfisher* at Her Majesty's Theatre in Melbourne. It was the final play he performed in before he passed away.

By this stage of his career it was well known that Frank was battling with a heavy drinking problem and, as Frank only had one line of dialogue in the second half of the play, he would hit the green room fridge fairly hard during intermission. He therefore needed a little assistance from the stage manager with his cue to go onstage, and this would involve standing Frank by the side of the stage and having a casual conversation with him until it was time for him to go on and say his one line. The stage manager would whisper the line to Frank, which was something like, 'Would madam like any more tea?' and then give him a gentle push, whereby Frank would walk straight on and repeat the line of dialogue. One particular night, Frank had got up there a little early and they were chatting away just after Frank had received his prompt when he asked, 'What are you doing tomorrow,' The stage manager replied, 'I'm going to Frankston,' and pushed Frank on. Frank promptly walked onstage and offered, 'I'm going to Frankston.' Not much you can do with that, really.

Yeah, nah, it was a
PRETTY BAD GIG

When comedians are asked to relate strange and troublesome performances, gigs involving footy clubs are right up there in the 'Jesus, did what happened really just happen?' category.

From struggling suburban clubs through to the wealthiest AFL teams, football club functions can vary greatly in terms of audience, venue, entertainment budget, and quality of the dim sims. Judging by the stories here, the one constant is that, at some stage, the gig is going to become all fucked up, and it's not always the comedian's fault.

Brad Oakes and Dave O'Neil were scheduled to perform on the same bill at a comedy night in the outer suburbs of Melbourne. When they arrived at the gig, the club president said to Dave, 'Yeah, can youse do some topical footy jokes as part of your comedy routine tonight?'

Dave is the first person to admit he really knows nothing about football, but the news from that week had followed the story of an AFL footballer, Lance Whitnall, who had been sent off to a weight loss camp. Football is a big deal in Melbourne, and anyone who had caught a snippet of news coverage that week would have been aware of Lance's weight battle, so that was the topical footy material that Dave decided to tackle. Now it just so happened that the football club that the show was in that night was the club where Lance Whitnall had played all of his junior football before rising to the rank of AFL player for Carlton. Dave should have realised that, because the wall behind the stage was a virtual Lance Whitnall shrine of honour, filled with many large photos, medals and trophies.

When Dave went onstage and launched into his routine of Lance Whitnall fat jokes, he was oblivious to the fact that he was standing in front of the 'Shrine of Lance' and that he was laying into the football club's favourite son. Dave was giving it the old, 'They say that Lance is in good shape now ... it's just that the shape he is in is a very *round* shape ... I'm not saying Lance is fat, but his driver's licence photo was taken with Google Earth ...' and so on. Now Dave has done these kinds of jokes for years, but usually about himself, and they work quite well when done in a self-deprecating way. But on this occasion, the room started to go very quiet, and this is why: the audience at this function was all men. There was only one woman in the whole place and she was stationed at the rear of the room behind a small deep fryer, preparing the dim sims. She was small and focused and had a look of underlying strength about her. She was well known around the club, as she had volunteered there for years, running the canteen, selling raffle tickets and barking orders that were obeyed by even the toughest of footballers. She took no bullshit from anyone. She was also Lance Whitnall's mother.

Dave described what happened next as being like a scene from a Western. The room had fallen silent and the only sound was the gentle frying of a dozen dim sims, coming from the deep fryer at the rear of the room. As if by some strange, unspoken communication, the crowd slowly parted as Lance Whitnall's mum purposefully, but unhurriedly, walked around the dim sim table and headed towards the stage, holding a pair of tongs.

The only thing missing from this impending showdown was a small, toothless cowboy with a large hat and a Southern accent saying, 'There's a gunna be an ass whuppin'!' before diving into a barrel.

Lance's mum reached the front of the room and stopped in front of the stage.

'You!' she gestured towards Dave with the tongs. 'How dare you come here, into *my* football club and insult my son!'

Dave said, 'Ahhh –'

'You think about where you are and what you say, 'cause I'll be watching you, sonny!' lectured Mrs Whitnall.

Spontaneous applause broke out from the crowd as she turned and walked back to the now slightly overcooked dim sims.

Dave O'Neil living the dream. Is it hot in here, or is it just me? *(James Peniidis)*

After the show had finished, the club president got up to finish the night and announced, rather underwhelmingly, 'Well that's it for the comedians – they weren't very good were they?'

A few minutes later Brad went over to him to arrange for him and Dave to get paid. As the president handed over the cheque to Brad he said gruffly, 'Do you blokes want to make a donation to the past players fund?' The answer to some questions can only be 'yes', and this was one of those questions. Brad said, 'Yes, of course,' while he was actually thinking, 'Ah, no, not really,' then he wondered how much he should give towards a past players fund. He got out his wallet, looked at his available cash and handed over a ten-dollar note to the president just as Dave walked up.

'What's going on?' asked Dave, thinking that maybe their pay had been docked and they both had to pay ten bucks back, or possibly that Brad was about to receive a quick hand job from the president.

Brad explained about the past players fund and asked if Dave would like to donate any money to it. Dave thought, sure, he could give ten bucks like Brad had done and then handed over a $50 note, expecting to get $40 change. The president pocketed the $50 and said, 'Oh thanks, mate, that's very generous!' while shooting Brad a dark look that said, 'Good one, tightarse!'

Ten bucks indeed.

Greg Fleet arrived at Lawrence Mooney's house one afternoon in a distressed state, following a gig; he had just done a pre-match function at Hawthorn Football Club. Fleety was wearing the smart, grey woollen suit that was his standard outfit for corporate gigs; he had thought it was best to look sharp for the straight-laced, affluent types that usually populate Hawthorn's match day events. However, when he arrived at Lawrence's house that winter afternoon, Fleety's smart suit had a large, damp stain down the front of it. Fleety's gig for the Hawthorn faithful had not gone well that day.

After struggling through ten minutes of material that was not getting much from the crowd, a pompous-looking gent, dressed appropriately in tweed, mounted the stage, approached Greg and said in a haughty voice, 'How dare you!' before promptly throwing his glass of red wine all over Fleety. Throwing red wine over someone at a Hawthorn function while saying the words, 'How dare you' is, I believe, just above calling someone a 'frightful bounder', and slightly worse than challenging someone's private school credentials. Lucky it wasn't a Collingwood function, or Fleety may have been dead.

One time at a footy club, Lawrence was introduced like this: 'The comedian that we wanted to have on tonight couldn't make it because his mum's sick. So here's ... ah ... sorry, I've forgotten his name.' A few minutes into the gig, Lawrence was struggling to get much response, when a bloke yelled out, 'I wish it was *your* mum who was sick!'

Furry funny man Dave Callan got a call from a comedian mate who asked him if he would like to come and do a spot at a footy club break-up night. Dave told him, 'I think that question can be answered by what I was doing when you rang me, which was playing a strategy game on my PC involving re-creating one of Hannibal's victories against the Carpathians ... while wearing a Doctor Who t-shirt.' In other words, footy is not really Dave's thing. He doesn't have anything against footy players, or the game itself, he told his friend, it's just that he thought those at the footy club, and Dave himself, would have a better time if he didn't do the gig. Fair enough. But the friend on the phone wouldn't take no for an answer.

'Aw, come on,' he begged, 'It's only just up the road from you.'

'No,' said Dave.

'You only have to do 20 minutes,' said his mate.

'I said no,' replied Dave.

'They're paying cash in hand,' his mate pleaded.

'Cash in hand, you say,' said Dave, thoughtfully. 'I could do with a few more Doctor Who t-shirts,' he pondered. 'Hmm, maybe I could juice up the old PC and get a bit more detail on the Carpathians' faces as I stab them to death.'

Dave agreed to do the gig.

It was on a Sunday afternoon, and Dave knew it was going to be a tough gig when he arrived to find all the adults drunk, and kids running all over the stage. By the way, 'kids running on a stage' is another warning sign that should be added to the list of signs of a potential shit gig. Dave's contact from the club, who was organising the gig, introduced himself as 'Stevo, but everyone calls me Macca'. Add to the list of shit gig warning signs 'blokes who have two nicknames organising the gig'.

While we're on the subject, is there a sporting club anywhere in the world that does not have some bloke called Macca? I'm sure you could call up a local mountain goat polo club in the Himalayas, ask to speak to Macca and get the answer, 'Yes, of course! As soon as he finishes milking the yak,' or whatever the Himalayan slang term is for having a wank.

Anyway, this Macca must have seen the initial look of panic on Dave's face, because he immediately said to him, 'Ah, here's your cash now,' and handed him a couple of hundred, which Dave put in his pocket.

Macca said, 'Okay, we're just gonna draw the raffle, and then you can go on after that.'

Macca got on the sound system, which Dave noticed was of very poor quality. He thought it sounded like Macca was ordering drive-though at, somewhat ironically, Macca's. Dave was contemplating just pulling the gig, but of course he had the cash in his pocket and couldn't help thinking of the highly detailed Carpathians being trampled by Hannibal's war elephants, which changed his mind.

With the raffle draw over, Macca said, 'Okay, are you right?'

Dave asked, 'Yeah, could you please go on and get the room

quietened down a bit before I start?'

'Nuh,' said Macca.

'Could you at least get the kids off the stage?' asked Dave.

Finally Macca agreed to get the noisy room quiet before he introduced Dave, so he got on the microphone and, to no one in particular, started quietly saying, 'Shaddup ... shaddup ... shaddup ...' He aimed his 'shaddups' at various different parts of the room and would get one part quiet then move onto the next section, and then the next. Meanwhile the first group would start talking again. It was like he was doing a plate-spinning routine, and he kept on having to come back and keep quieting the sections of the crowd.

Dave Callan. Even chicken wire wouldn't help at some gigs
(James Penlidis)

'Come on people,' he pleaded. 'We've already paid this bloke out of the raffle money, could youse just shaddup?'

He got about half the crowd quiet, which was the best he was going to do, then he said, 'Okay everyone, we've got a comedian coming on now. He reckons he's been on the telly but I haven't seen him. Anyway, here he is, Dave Callahan.'

Dave went on and it was just awful. People were talking, kids were running around all over the place and the sound system was hopeless, so Dave did about ten minutes and then got off.

Macca came running over and said, 'What are you doing? Why didn't you do your full 20 minutes?'

Dave replied, 'Well the sound system you've provided is very poor and sounded worse than the one at Flinders Street Station. I didn't think the crowd really wanted to hear me do another ten minutes of train announcements. Plus you only got half of them quiet before you brought me on. They couldn't even understand me well enough to heckle me, and that's why I only did half of the time.'

'Well do you want to give back half of the money then?' Macca asked.

'Ah ... no, not really,' Dave replied, 'I want to give back half the money like you wanted to introduce me.'

'All right then,' said Macca, 'Come outside.'

Along the way, Macca grabbed a giant, mean-looking man and brought him outside as well. Meanwhile Dave was trying to think of more reasons to not give back half of the money.

'Look,' Dave said, 'the gig was fucked up from the start. They were extremely challenging circumstances. I've come all the way out here –' he lived just down the street – 'you didn't provide the right environment for me to perform in, and that's half the work right there, so that's why I only did half of the work.'

Macca said to the giant standing next to him, 'Well, what do you reckon?'

'Give half the money back,' he grunted.

Dave could see no way out, so he reluctantly dug in his pocket and gave half of the money back, and with it went his dreams of a new Doctor Who t-shirt and upgraded video card for his PC.

Koo Wee Rup is a small town on the far south-eastern edge of Melbourne – though with the suburban sprawl of the Victorian capital reaching epic proportions, Koo Wee Rup is pretty much now an outer suburb of Cranbourne, which is pretty much an outer suburb of Melbourne. So we can accurately say that Koo Wee Rup is an outer suburb of an outer suburb.

Dave Thornton had a Koo Wee Rup experience that still sends a shiver down his spine when he hears the three words – Koo, Wee and Rup – spoken in that order. Not that you'd ever be likely to hear the words 'Koo' and 'Rup' without 'Wee' in the middle. Dave's Koo Wee Rup experience was shared with his two comedian buddies Tom Siegert and Troy Kinne. Back when they were all starting out in comedy, they used to sell themselves as a comedy night package to footy clubs or sportsman's nights. They were all young and eager and were happy to do these gigs for a couple of hundred bucks each – $600 for an entire comedy show is pretty decent value, so they used to get a few of these shows all around Victoria.

The Koo Wee Rup Football Club gig was actually booked through a comedy agent who had organised everything for them. The boys were thinking, 'Wow, a gig booked by an agent! Next stop Hollywood!' They would be performing for the annual footy club fundraiser, and the boys found out that it had been compulsory for the players to attend the night, despite the Koo Wee Rup team being flogged by 15 goals in their game against the mighty Poowong Magpies that same afternoon. Despite the compulsory attendance, quite a few players had just simply refused to turn up, so the crowd was made up of about 20 players and ten of their girlfriends – none of them really in the mood for comedy. When the boys did these kinds of shows, they would rotate the order in which they went on. On this particular night, they were alternating their comedy spots with a cover band who specialised in Bryan Adams and Nickelback songs. These Koo Wee Rup folks were really gluttons for punishment.

Troy Kinne was the first one up to try his comedy stylings on the sad and sorry Koo Wee Ruppites, but his usually solid material got absolutely nothing. Dave and Tom were standing backstage listening to the deafening silence that was greeting Troy, and they were growing more and more apprehensive at what lay in store for them. After about 15 minutes, Troy had given all he could and retreated backstage defeated, leaving the stage to the opening chords of 'Summer of 69' as the band struck up their next set.

Tom was the next lucky cab off the comedy rank. Tom is a bit of a cross between Carl Barron and Elliot Goblet – very droll with a laid-back delivery, and very funny. He does jokes like this, 'My first car and my first sexual experience were both old escorts …'

This night, however, he got nothing from the crowd and came off with his tail between his legs. Finally, it was Dave's turn to get onstage and perform for the unhappy, bored and now very drunk crowd. He did his first three jokes, which were met with silence, then decided to pull out his never-fail Dave Hughes impression, which also got nothing. He blamed Dave Hughes for not being more famous. He stared out at the 30 or so sad souls in the crowd, decided that he just couldn't face it any more and simply said, 'Look, I'm sorry, but that's it guys. I think you'll enjoy the band more than me trying to tell jokes, so it's good night from me.' So after three jokes and a Dave Hughes impression, the show was over for Dave Thornton. He headed backstage and into the dressing room, where he was met by the gloomy faces of Troy and Tom. At least the gig was over, they could put it behind them and never speak of Koo Wee Rup ever again. The next thing he saw and heard was the coach of the footy club storming through the dressing room door shouting, 'What the fuck was that?'

Dave said, 'Mate, they weren't having any fun out there. If you're not happy with the time I did, just cut my pay. In fact, don't give me anything. I'm happy to just walk away from this gig and you keep the two hundred bucks.'

The coach said, 'What do you mean two hundred?'

'Two hundred for each of us, that's why it was six hundred all up,' said Dave.

'Six hundred?' asked the coach, 'I've already paid your agent, and it was eighteen hundred bucks, not six hundred!'

Dave's mind raced as he thought, 'That measly agent had charged the coach $1800 and kept $1200 for himself!' But Dave had bigger and more imminent problems than the greedy agent to contend with.

'The way I see it, you owe us six hundred bucks,' reasoned the coach.

'What?' exclaimed Dave.

'If we're docking your pay like you're telling us to, then you owe us six hundred bucks and you're not fucken leaving until we get it,' said the coach, who now had some of the larger lads of the footy club backing him up.

None of the boys had anywhere near $600 to pay the coach, but Dave bought some time by saying they had to call the agent to try and sort it all out. The agent was mightily pissed off that the total fee had been revealed, but he was safely tucked up in his dressing gown back in Melbourne, watching telly, and not facing an angry football team. Meanwhile Troy, who is a well built, barrel chested young man, was bouncing around Dave going, 'We can take 'em, we can fucken take 'em!' Now anyone who's ever seen Dave Thornton in a confronting situation before will tell you that unless it's going to break into a dance battle, he's probably not the bloke you want to go into a fight with.

'They are a drunk mob of angry country football players,' shouted Dave. 'We are most certainly not going to fucking well take 'em!'

The stand-off with the coach resumed, this time with a fresh batch of even larger looking lads standing behind him. The coach finally accepted that they were not going to get any money from

WHAT, AND GIVE UP **SHOWBIZ?**

(Rusty Berther)

the boys that night, so he said, 'You all better fuck off out of here right now, and don't show your faces here ever again, or we are going to kick the shit of you!'

They didn't need to be told twice, and the players formed a threatening 'guard of honour' to escort the boys out to their car.

It was like it was a funeral procession and Dave, Tom and Troy were the pallbearers at the death of their own gig.

Never work with children or ANIMALS OR JUGGLERS

'Never work with children or animals' is a line credited to the great American comedian WC Fields. The most obvious reason for this saying is that animals and children have an innate cuteness and innocence that even the most experienced performer cannot possibly compete with. Add to that the fact that at some point while a child or animal is on stage, the surprise appearance of bodily functions is highly probable, sidelining any of the performers' material, even that of the highest quality.

I've never had to work with an animal onstage, but I have had a show disrupted by one during a spot at the legendary Melbourne comedy theatre restaurant the Last Laugh. It was with a typically tough Friday night crowd – a mixture of bucks' nights, hen's nights and a few office parties thrown in for good measure.

As the evening progressed, a table of army blokes on one side of the room had been making their presence felt, while on the other side of the room, one of the bucks' night tables had been giving the army blokes a run for their money.

During our performance, I had noticed portions of the crowd were occasionally looking up at the ceiling and becoming increasingly distracted. There was pointing and laughing, and a few women let out what could be described as 'startled shrieks'. The Last Laugh was in a very old building with quite a high ceiling, and this was a good thing, as we soon realised the cause of the commotion. One of the dickheads on the bucks' table had released a bat, which was now circling around the room. As it was quite dark in the audience, you could only see the bat intermittently, when it flew through a spotlight or was low enough to give someone a sudden fright. The distraction was too much, and we had to stop the show until things settled down.

Let's just go back to that bit about one of the dickheads releasing a bat into the room. Now, when most people are preparing to go out for the evening, they would do a quick mental checklist of the things they might need during the night: keys, money, phone, etc., and off they go and have a top time. I struggle to comprehend what kind of brainless peanut includes 'live bat' on the list of things that he believes may contribute to the enjoyment of the group at some point during their night out. I don't quite know how the night escalated, but when I came upstairs from the dressing room after the show, the two opposing tables of knuckleheads had moved out into the foyer, with words flying and fists ready. The manager, Fred, was off to one side with the 'leaders' of the bucks' table and the army blokes, trying to calm things down.

'Look, mate, we've had a pretty good night, and I'm sorry about the bat, but those army pricks are just going too far. Personally, I'm not into fightin', but if it's on, I'm happy to,' explained the bucks' table representative.

Fred did his job well and managed to talk the groups out of fighting each other. As the bucks' table bloke was leaving, he said to Fred, 'One more thing, tell the chef that the beans were undercooked.'

Fred later mentioned this to the chef who said, 'Beans? There were no beans on the menu tonight. I think he must be referring to the asparagus.'

NEVER WORK WITH CHILDREN OR ANIMALS OR JUGGLERS

In the early 1990s, when the Scaredies hadn't been around for very long, we were lucky enough to score a spot at one of the most highly sought-after gigs a comedy act could ever wish to play – an outdoor boy scout jamboree.

It was held on a large area of farmland about half an hour outside Ballarat, though it had been raining solidly for a week, so it was more accurate to say it was held on a large area of mud half an hour outside of Ballarat. The scouts were at the end of a week of tying knots, swapping badges, burning things and doing whatever else it is that scouts do on jamborees.

They had to do everything that they would normally do on a jamboree, except that they did it while being soaked to the skin. So I am pretty sure that they were thoroughly sick of behaving themselves and in no mood for sitting quietly and watching some entertainment.

We were sharing the bill with a comedian, a juggler and a Seventies cover band (remember it was 1992 and the Eighties weren't retro yet).

While we were standing backstage before the show, and being fairly fresh in the comedy and entertainment world, not to mention the boy scout jamboree world, the juggler was giving us performance advice, him being the most experienced entertainer there, and him being a juggler. He was saying things like, 'You gotta hit 'em hard and hit 'em fast. Take your chances early and it will pay off.'

Listening to the juggler, I was unsure if we were performing for the scouts or playing footy against them.

'And the one golden rule, guys: if they throw stuff, get off!'

We were suitably impressed. This juggler sounded like a real veteran, who had obviously had lots of stuff thrown at him before.

The comedian went on first and didn't do very well. To be fair, those 11-year-old scouts were a tough crowd: hardened and battle weary after a week in the rain and the mud, eating cold camp food and being away from their loved ones and video games. Something was ready to blow, which was okay for us, because the juggler was up next. He left the dressing room and headed up to the stage. John and I started tuning up and thinking about what songs we were going to do, when, after only a few minutes, the juggler burst back into the room completely covered with clumps of mud. There were clumps stuck all over his juggler costume and clinging to his fuzzy hair, as well as two perfectly aimed mud balls right on his face; one on his cheek and a large one on his forehead.

'They threw stuff! The little bastards threw stuff!'

We went on feeling nervous, and I could tell those little campers wanted to hurl mud at us, but just before we were introduced an enormous scout leader, who looked like a large Grizzly Adams, got on the mic and told them that if any more mud was thrown there would be severe consequences. Reduced badge swapping privileges or something like that. It worked, because we got through the gig unharmed, or at least unmuddied.

Brian Nankervis loves performing. When he is not co-producing, writing questions for and filming the rock nerdtacular quiz show *RocKwiz*, he can be found hosting trivia nights for football clubs or community groups, being the warm-up guy extraordinaire at other television shows, or getting out to do school shows. For schools, he brings out his avant-garde poet character, Raymond J Bartholomew, as well as doing some interactive drama pieces for a bit of fun.

Being an ex high school drama teacher, he knows that a group of uninterested students can be a tough crowd, and this was hammered home to him one Friday afternoon, after he found himself driving to an outer suburb of Geelong for a school show. He knew he was in for an interesting day when he parked his car in the street at the front of the school and a teacher came running out waving his arms and saying, 'Don't leave your car there! Didn't you see *A Current Affair* last night?'

'No, why?' asked Brian, a little startled.

'This street has just been voted the most dangerous street in Australia. Get back in your car and follow me so you can park in the school grounds.'

After moving his car, Brian went to the school's reception, introduced himself and said, 'I'm here to do a show for the Year 9s.'

'Tsk, good luck!' scoffed the receptionist.

Brian found a similar attitude in a few of the teachers he met once he got to the staff room.

'Ugh, Year 9? Good luck with that!'

'Geez, I wouldn't want to be in your shoes, mate.'

From their reactions, he might have been about to go and face a horde of grunting, aggressive Neanderthals, though, as many teachers would tell you, facing 180 Year 9s on a Friday afternoon is probably not that far off.

Brian began setting up for the show on the stage of the school hall, as the mass of sweaty, disillusioned Year 9s filed in, then slumped into the seats lined up facing the stage. Brian would have had trouble keeping their attention if he was a noisy thrash metal band fresh from the Triple J Top 100. The fact that he was a 40-something man doing experimental avant-garde poetry probably put him behind the eight ball somewhat. Despite teachers being strategically placed around the room, the students were poking each other, pulling each other's hair, and generally

WHAT, AND GIVE UP SHOWBIZ?

Raymond J Bartholomew contemplating the
intricacies of performing to Year 9 students
(James Penlidis)

doing what passes for distracted social interaction among 14 year olds.

If you are getting nothing from a crowd early on during a performance, you can easily fall into the 'go too hard too early' approach, and this is what Brian found himself doing in front of the uninterested students. During the first few minutes, he had noticed three rather scruffy-looking lads slouched right in the front row. They knew that they could not be seen by any of the teachers around the room, and whenever Brian looked at them they would silently and nastily mouth the words 'Fuck off'. These kids didn't think what Brian was doing was fun, or educational, or even boring. They just thought he was being ridiculous and stupid, and they wanted him to know how they felt.

Brian found himself getting unusually distracted by these boys, then he thought, 'No, I am an experienced professional, and I won't let them beat me.'

Sometimes it is interesting how small distractions can throw you off your game. Brian had thousands of live performances under his belt, and was confident in his own ability, but these three teenagers were really getting to him. He reacted to the audience's lack of response by going a bit harder in his own performance, overcompensating and using bigger actions, and probably more avant-garde-iness than the kids were ready for, but he was determined to see this gig through to the end.

His show had begun at 2 pm and it was supposed to last an hour. When you are struggling in front of a tough crowd, time can seem to go slowly, and when Brian took a quick look at his watch, he was horrified to see that it was only eight minutes past two. Always one to look on the bright side, he thought, 'At least my car isn't being broken into.'

There has recently been a rise in the popularity of comedy cruises, where a cruise ship will leave port for three or four days and people are essentially held captive within the confines of the ship, with no possible escape from comedians or comedy shows. Personally, I can't think of a worse way to spend three or four days. Only kidding, there are probably a few worse things.

Dave Callan performed on one of these cruises – a fact that he doesn't tell many people. You see, some comedians go for a week to entertain the troops in a Middle East warzone, and some go on a floating RSL for three days of buffets and trying to avoid weird comedy fans.

When taking the booking, Dave was told he just had to do two performances of the same 40-minute show on one night of the cruise and that was it. It sounded pretty sweet until the organisers tried to squeeze out a few extra 'surprise' gigs once he was on board. Because there were a few days at sea at the beginning of the cruise, Dave was asked if he could perform at a kids' show – for no extra fee.

It was Dave's first time on a cruise ship, he was having a good time and the people were very nice, plus he wanted to be invited back, so while he wanted to say no, he agreed to doing the kids' show, thinking it would be just like a normal show, without the swear words.

When Dave and the other comedians got to the venue for the show, the scene was utter bedlam. There was yelling and screaming and unfocused running around – and that was just from the comedians, who were not used to the idea of entertaining children. The kids were even worse.

Dave started the show and quickly realised that he was going to have to do a bit more to entertain the kids than just take out all the 'fucks' from his routine, and that the kids were probably not going to get *all* the references. He thought that he could easily kill some time with a little question and answer session with some of the kids.

'Are there any questions?' he boomed in his thick, Scottish brogue.

A kid who was about six years of age and sitting down the front immediately shot his hand into the air.

'What's your name?' asked Dave.

'Lachlan!' shouted the confident little fellow.

'And what is your question, Lachlan?'

'Um, do you ever do wee in your own pants?' he shouted.

Dave paused, to laughter from the other kids, and said, 'No, I don't, Lachlan. I know I may look homeless, but I do not wee in my own pants, but thank you for your question. Are there any more questions?'

A girl who was sitting next to Lachlan thrust her hand up. She was slightly younger than Lachlan and obviously his sister. 'I have a question,' she said.

'What's your name, young lady?'

'Holly!' she shouted, exactly like Lachlan.

'And what is your question?' asked Dave.

'Do you ever do poo on your own face?' she asked, giggling.

'What the hell is wrong with your family?' Dave asked both of them. This was the first morning of day one of the cruise and it was already turning a bit weird for Dave, but he sighed and attempted to answer the question and get on with the show.

'I know I look like I live in a cardboard box, but no, Holly, I do not do that on my own face.'

The parents who were watching this show were having a blast, and then Dave added, 'How do you even do that on your own face, anyway? I mean, I once did some nude yoga and accidentally tea bagged myself, but you kids are just weird.'

Dave Callan did no more kids' shows during that cruise, nor has he done any since.

A spectacular event was planned for the launch of a new model of automobile for an Australian car manufacturer. I won't say which particular Australian car manufacturer was planning this spectacular launch, but as there are only about four companies still making cars in Australia, and that list is shrinking, and this launch involved a lion, you score no points for working out who was hosting the event.

It was Holden, by the way, but that is irrelevant because the only fact that matters here is that this story involves a lion. Not the lion-shaped red thing on the Holden logo, but an actual live lion.

The launch was scheduled to be held on a warm summer evening in Melbourne, and on the afternoon of the event, the venue was buzzing with staging and sound crews, riggers, lighting operators and various technicians setting up for what was to be the glamorous unveiling of a new car in front of 500 or so suitably impressed car dealers, and some journalists and photographers unlucky enough to have been assigned to the 'car launch job'.

The gleaming new car was set in the centre of the stage on a rotating circular podium. Various stage hands were up ladders, hanging the fancy curtains that were to conceal it until the reveal, and various whistles and bells were being prepared for the imminent rehearsal, when the call went out to all of the workers, 'Stand by for the arrival of the lion.'

I imagine the creative meeting of the event planners, where a guy with sunglasses placed casually on his mullet haircut and wearing a shoulder-padded jacket with the sleeves pulled up said something along the lines of, 'Okay, guys, we'll have some curtains surrounding the car, and a smoke machine with lasers shining through the smoke, yeah that will make it look great! And we should have some really loud rock music blaring, what a top idea! Hmm, it's missing something, though. Something that goes well with smoke and lasers and loud rock music … of course … a lion!'

So the lion, which was contained inside a large wooden crate, was driven into the venue on a forklift and positioned underneath the stage. A tunnel had been constructed that led to a ramp with an entrance to the front of the stage, and a tall perspex barrier had been erected around the front of the stage to prevent any unforeseen lion–audience interaction. The plan was that as the new car was unveiled, the lion would make its way along the tunnel, up the ramp and onto the stage, then give a few loud roars, which I guess would somehow enhance the desirability of the car and make all the car dealers extra-eager to sell it.

The organisers of the event had told the lion's handler that it was important to get the lion to roar. However, getting a real lion to roar on cue is not such an easy thing to do. It's a simple idea if you are using a robotic lion, or perhaps two humans in a lion suit, but in showbiz, there is only one way to ensure that a lion is going to let off a few roars – you starve it. The downside of that is of course that you will then have to contend with a hungry lion. But as long as you get a few well-timed roars out of the poor thing, I guess it's worth the risk of losing a few lanky promotional models. Plenty more where they came from, right?

With the lion in position under the stage, the rehearsal began with lasers, smoke and the opening riff of 'TNT' blaring through the ample sound system. Lasers, smoke and 'TNT' may be a combination of audio and visual stimuli that brings natural excitement to a group of car dealers, but to a starving lion, it made it feel like it had been trapped in a wooden cage next to a brushfire at an AC/DC concert – not the usual conditions you find out on the African savannah.

The lion promptly kicked out the back of the cage and ran along the tunnel up onto the stage. It looked around, and appropriately let out a load roar, which sent the workers flying in all directions, up ladders, behind curtains and through the first exit door they came to. The lion, probably still trying to get away from the loud music and smoke, took one look at the perspex safety barrier, ran towards it and crashed through into the seats of the large auditorium, roaming up and down the aisles and possibly looking for a promotional model or two to chew on. The call went out for the lion's handler, who had been one of the first to shoot up the tallest ladder he could find. He was told in no uncertain terms to get the hell down and retrieve his tranquilliser gun to calm the unfortunate beast. This he did, though with limited success, as the first shot missed, leaving him with only one more shot. The second shot was successful, but the lion didn't get knocked out by the dart, and was merely calmed and remained awake and looking around while sitting peacefully in one of the aisles. Still, none of the workers were prepared to chance going back to work, so the call went out to the Melbourne Zoo for more assistance. It was nearly an hour before help arrived in the form of another dart gun in the hands of an experienced helper, who promptly and accurately got the lion into an unconscious state.

A call was put out to all of the workers so that the stage could be returned to some semblance of non-lion normality, though after a quick head count, there were still ten technicians missing. They were eventually found, all ten of them, crammed into the new car on the stage, where they had jammed themselves at the first appearance of the lion and where they had remained for the past hour.

I've played EVERYWHERE, MAN

I've been a fan of Johnny Cash's *At Folsom Prison* album ever since I can remember. It was on high rotation whenever my mother hosted her friends over at our place for games nights. My brother and sister and I were allowed to stay up late on those nights, as endless games of canasta, five hundred and Yahtzee were played by the adults, while the kids got to choose the music from mum's battered collection of country and pop vinyl albums, before inevitably being welcomed to join in on the games. There was Neil Diamond's *Hot August Night*, Jim Reeves, Patsy Cline, Lefty Frizzell, plenty of the Statler Brothers, and about 50 Charlie Pride albums. We kids used to make fun of the simplicity of the country music, unaware that the uncomplicated melodies and down-to-earth subjects of love, life and death would come to influence us in our later musical lives.

Johnny Cash's *At Folsom Prison* was our favourite. I was fascinated by the sounds of the prisoners cheering and shouting whenever Cash sang a lyric about prison, murder or drugs, and many times I sat and stared at the photograph on the back cover of his captive audience with their hardened faces, denim shirts and flattop haircuts, wondering what crimes they had committed that condemned them to being forced to watch the concert. It was influential stuff for a young lad and I remember thinking, 'One day I am going to write songs, just like Johnny Cash; and

(Rusty Berther)

perform a gig in a prison, just like Johnny Cash; and I am going to get myself an addiction to pills, just like Johnny Cash.' I didn't actually think any of those things, but I did once get to do a show in a prison.

At a friend's party I met a very interesting woman who was in charge of a special youth unit at a prison outside Melbourne. The unit was set up for around 40 prisoners between the ages of 18 and 24, who predominately were serving their first sentence in a maximum security prison. The prisoners in the youth unit were separated from the main prison population, and there was a strong emphasis on developing positive social behaviour, minimising the risk of self-harm and prevention of re-offending. To remain in the youth unit, the prisoners had to complete various educational and personal development programs such as drug and alcohol awareness, basic schooling, and anger management. If the young prisoners stuffed up once, they were sent straight back into the main prison population, so they rarely stuffed up.

So when I was chatting to Kim, the youth development officer at the prison, I made a reference to the Johnny Cash prison performances and she said, 'You should come in and do a show.'

A show in a real prison, just like Johnny Cash?

Show me to the pills and you've got yourself a deal!

We spoke on the phone a few days later, and once I had confirmed that the prisoners had all completed their anger management courses, we agreed on a date and my childhood goal of performing in a prison was a step closer to becoming a reality.

A few weeks later, John and I drove out of Melbourne towards the prison – Johnny Cash on the stereo and sweaty palms on the steering wheel. I actually wasn't feeling too nervous about anything bad happening to me in prison, because in preparation I had re-watched *The Shawshank Redemption* and a few old repeats of *Prisoner*. Surely it was merely a case of being wary while showering and staying away from the room with the ironing boards in it and there would be no trouble.

We had to take all our own equipment into the prison for the show, including a small sound system, as well as our guitars. We had decided not to wear our matching sparkly suits, as 'overt displays of flamboyance' was number two in the 'Things to avoid when visiting a prison' pamphlet that we had been sent a few days before.

Everything that we took in for the show had to be itemised, the serial numbers recorded, then passed through a metal detector. It was just like being at the airport about to depart on a holiday, except this holiday wouldn't really meet your pre-holiday expectations:

'Hang on a sec, I am pretty sure there was nothing in the

brochure about getting "shivved in the guts during exercise time" ...'

After signing in, going through passport control and picking up our duty free, the prison officers thoroughly searched our guitars and speakers for anything we were likely to be smuggling into the prison.

I asked one of the officers what they were looking for.

'You'd be amazed at the type of things that visitors try to smuggle into prison,' he said, with a serious look, 'mobile phones, drugs ...'

'Birthday cakes containing concealed files?' I offered.

His expression didn't change, '... weapons, syringes.'

I said cheerfully, 'Well, my friend, the only thing we're smuggling into the prison today is laughter, and the only thing we'll leave behind are smiles.'

After he strip-searched me, we gathered our equipment, loaded it onto a trolley and continued further into the prison. We were let through two imposing steel doors with tiny glass windows and emerged into a large central outdoor area.

It was here I saw my first real-life prisoner. He didn't look any different from someone you would meet on the street, and he was dressed in the standard prison gear of a white t-shirt, green trousers, Dunlop Volleys and neck tattoo. He was pushing a trolley loaded with dishes and crockery, and even though he looked like a regular person, I felt a little uneasy, so I traded him some cigarettes for a sharpened toothbrush and a porno mag and we continued on.

I don't know what it is like for a woman, but I reckon men think a lot about what it would be like to be in jail. There are so many books, movies and television shows that depict what life may or may not be like on the inside, and most of it is not very nice. Then you read about men who make a bad decision, like drink driving or punching someone who dies, and they end up in prison, just like that. So to be in a real prison for the first time was a sobering experience. Looking around, the rows of two-storey buildings linked by covered walkways reminded me of being back at high school, only with more razor wire and rifles.

We entered the building that housed the Youth Unit with our prison guard escort and trolley laden with speakers and guitars. The double-storey building housed 40 cells, and their heavy, dark green doors all faced on to a central common area about 30 metres long. There were a few tables and chairs in this area and two of the inmates were playing table tennis up one end of the room. There was a staircase at each end, and two prison guards kept on eye on everything from a raised circular enclosure in the centre of the room that reminded me of an information desk at a suburban shopping centre. I introduced myself to one of the guards and ignored the urge to ask him for directions to the food court, and instead asked him where we should set up for our show. He grunted and gestured to the floor at one end of the building and we wheeled our gear over and proceeded to set up.

In all the thousands of shows that the Scaredies performed we had never, ever walked into our performance area with our equipment on a trolley and then spent 20 minutes setting up while the audience stood and sat around watching us. Doing that at a primary school would be a little unsettling, let alone doing it for the first time in your life in a prison while 40 prisoners milled around or stared at you in silence with their arms folded. I was feeling very self-conscious and nervous but was trying to act tough and nonchalant, which was difficult due to my habit of whistling cheerfully whenever I get nervous. I tried to imagine what it would be like to be in the prison all the time, and suddenly to have two blokes come in and start setting up musical equipment for a show. I could sense that most of the onlookers were interested but didn't want to seem too enthusiastic about it.

One of the inmates came over for a chat. He looked so young to me – probably about 18 years old – and he asked about my guitar and the mixing desk. All I wanted to ask him was what he had done to end up here. Eventually I asked him how long he was in for, which I later learned was the appropriate question to ask instead of, 'What are you in for?' He was surprisingly articulate and honest in his answers. He was six months into a three-year sentence. He had been a promising footballer, then had got addicted to speed, which led to robberies and assault. He said that was all behind him now and he couldn't wait to get out, and I believed he was telling the truth. While we were talking, a nasty looking little fellow cruised by within earshot and muttered, 'You suckhole,' to my new friend, who replied loudly and aggressively, 'Why don't you go and fuck yourself, cockhead!'

'Hey, cool it!' shouted one of the guards from the information desk.

So, how's that anger management course coming along? I wondered. I really didn't want to be the catalyst for any bad vibes and have any inmates getting all stabby on us.

When it was time to start the show, it was the most underwhelming beginning of any show I've ever done. Once we knew that sound was coming out of the speakers and the guitars were on, I looked at John, raised my eyebrows, he shrugged his shoulders, and off we went.

I thought it might be funny to start the gig off like the Johnny Cash Folsom Prison show, so I stepped up to the microphone and in my best Johnny Cash voice said, 'Hello, we're the Scared Weird Little Guys.' Then I played the opening riff to 'Folsom Prison Blues' and, strangely, those young prisoners didn't react like Johnny's audience had – with applause and cheers of delight; stunned indifference is how I would describe their reaction. They obviously hadn't heard of Johnny Cash, and they certainly hadn't heard of us. There were about 30 of them slumped in chairs with their arms folded and the laughs weren't coming easily. Not necessarily because they didn't find things funny, but again I sensed they were feeling very self-conscious about showing their reactions. After a few songs they settled in and we all relaxed a bit. The best responses were when we asked them to give us songs that we attempted to do in different musical styles. Most of their requests were for obscure hip hop artists that we'd never heard of and they seemed to enjoy thinking they'd stumped us. After the show, it didn't seem to be such an issue for the inmates to come and chat with us, and we stayed for another two hours. I was struck by the diversity of the backgrounds of the young men I spoke with that day. Not only ethnically, but also how they were from all social classes and financial backgrounds, university educated to primary school dropouts. It was a real eye-opener for me and I remain thoroughly impressed with the whole set up they have there, particularly their success with the anger management program.

So I achieved my dream of performing in a prison. And now Johnny Cash and I share something in common, though thankfully not an addiction to pills.

At the height of *The Comedy Company*'s enormous popularity, Glenn Robbins was asked to go over to New Zealand for a gig on the South Island. He was asked if he could appear as one of the show's best-known characters – the bumbling antiquarian Uncle Arthur. He had performed this character a number of times before, so he had a bit of a routine for Uncle Arthur, plus the rambling nature of the character easily allowed for improvisation.

Glenn Robbins as Uncle Arthur
(James Penlidis)

And just why was Uncle Arthur being flown over the Tasman? To judge an Uncle Arthur lookalike competition at a local horseracing track.

On the morning of the gig, Glenn got dressed up in his Uncle Arthur costume – old, ill-fitting suit, fake grey moustache, thick glasses, and his hair plastered down over his forehead. As he was driven in to the racetrack, he saw a large grandstand and hoped he wasn't going to be plonked in front of it and an audience of a few thousand uninterested punters. That wouldn't have been much fun. But it's okay, because it was much worse than that: the stage had been set up in the centre of the oval-shaped track, at least a couple of hundred metres away from the closest audience member. As Glenn approached the stage, he could see that it was surrounded by a few dozen Uncle Arthurs, all patiently awaiting the arrival of their leader.

He got up onstage and welcomed the first of the Uncle Arthurs up in typical Uncle Arthur style: 'Aw yeah, er, righto, okay then,' or words to that effect.

The first Uncle Arthur walked onstage and said into the microphone, 'Aw yeah, er, righto, okay then,' or words to that effect, except in a New Zealand accent. This process was basically repeated for the next ten minutes until the line of Uncle Arthurs was exhausted and a winner was crowned. It didn't really matter who won, as the audience were so far away, all of the Uncle Arthurs looked pretty much identical – including Glenn.

I'm sure he could have gone and held up a bookie and the true culprit could never have been found. That would be some court case, though.

'How do the defendants plead?'

'Aw yeah, er, righto, okay then.'

The Linden Tree was a quaint little bar-restaurant in St Kilda, renowned for two things – being open really late and stabbings. Apart from that it really didn't have much going for it. The Linden Tree was your last stop when all other venues had closed and for some reason you wanted to continue your night out while increasing your chances of violent affray.

The linden – the tree, not the venue – is a Slovenian symbol of friendship, love and loyalty; three things that I never experienced while in the St Kilda Linden Tree. The venue was run by an elderly German couple. They looked very similar to each other and were only distinguishable by the wife's large apron, as they both had the same rotund body shape and similar moustaches. They would not have been out of place as the proprietors of a fairytale gingerbread house, were it not for the wife's menacing mono-brow and permanent scowl.

She would bark orders in a foreign language, presumably German, to her husband and to the staff. The husband rarely spoke; his demeanour was that of an obedient slave whose spirit had long been broken, and his night was usually spent trudging slowly back and forth from the kitchen carrying bowls of bratwurst and cabbage to the eclectic mix of punters.

The Linden Tree certainly had atmosphere. It had a low ceiling, was always very smoky and was crammed with tables and chairs made of ancient, thick wood. It had dim lighting (probably thankfully) and a heavy fug dominated the interior, though that was probably due more to the bratwurst and cabbage than anything else. A small stage was set into one corner and a diverse line-up of bands, duos and solo singers could be found playing there on any night of the week.

In the late 1980s my sister Sherry and I had been getting a bit of work around town with our sweet-singing country duo. We would often busk at the Camberwell or Esplanade markets and get the occasional pub gig where our sibling-blended harmonies and simple country repertoire of Patsy, Johnny and Hank songs would usually delight the audience. I don't quite remember how it came about that we found ourselves doing the midnight to 3 am spot on a Wednesday night at the Linden Tree, but I do remember that we had to play three 45-minute sets.

The clientele of drunken lonely guys, junkies and St Kilda rock and roll types out for a post-gig beverage largely ignored us, but I noticed there were a few toes tapping and it certainly wasn't going badly.

During the first set I looked over to the bar and saw the German lady standing unmoving, staring at us with a stern look and a slight glistening on her moustache. I remember thinking as we were singing a song in three-four waltz time that she would probably be enjoying the music because, you know, lots of German music is in three-four waltz time. After the first set I ventured up to the bar to get a drink and was confronted by Sergeant Schulzette.

'Hi,' I said, smiling. 'Can I get a beer, please?'

'No,' she said..

'No?'

I'VE PLAYED EVERYWHERE, MAN

Rusty and Sherry Sue. Sweet-singing, good-timing country duo. Avoided being stabbed in some of Melbourne's dodgiest venues
(Rusty Berther)

'You must buy,' she shot back. 'You have money?' Her steely eyes pierced deep into my brain. I felt I should be confessing to being a spy or divulging the whereabouts of Allied munitions dumps or something.

'Oh, okay then,' I said, and paid the 12 cents or whatever it cost for a beer back then.

Needless to say I didn't go and talk to her again until we had finished the gig and were packing up and I had to see someone about getting paid. I started heading back behind the bar, but was cut off by the unfriendly fraulein as she appeared from behind a fridge.

'So we've finished,' I began, 'and we need to get pai –'

'Zis iz not muzik!' she shouted, gesturing to the stage. 'Zis iz rubbish!' She actually put her hands on my shoulders and shook me. 'You are rubbish!' she shouted into my face.

I was speechless, to say the least, but I managed to softly say, 'Er, about our pay ...' She stormed off and left her husband to deal with us. He gave us $150, which was $30 less than we were supposed to get, but I didn't want to hang around and take it up with the fraulein.

I don't think I have ever been as scared by anyone as much as I was scared of her.

On one of his first trips to the UK, Wil Anderson scored a gig in a Manchester nightclub. The venue wasn't really suited for a comedy show; it was just a nightclub with chairs in it, and a room that has an overwhelming odour of vomit, regret and bad decisions is not the perfect place to perform comedy.

The emcee told Wil that the audiences in this particular room had a quirk. He said, 'Look mate, the crowds are a bit weird here. They won't laugh at your first three jokes, but if they're good jokes they'll trust you, and then they'll laugh at your fourth one and you'll be fine from then onwards.'

The emcee got up onstage and introduced Wil by saying, 'This next act is from Australia,' and the entire audience joined in on an extremely loud chorus of 'Boo!' Probably because around that point in time, the Australian cricket team was smacking the Poms in yet another Ashes series, which is fine for Australian cricket fans, but not so fine in terms of Anglo-Australo comedy audience relations.

Wil heard the boos and thought, 'I am going to have to do my absolute best three jokes to begin the set if I have any chance of getting to that fabled fourth joke and comedy success in this dodgy Manchester nightclub.'

He opened with his 'toilet door graffiti' joke, which he had started his set with for years and which goes like this:

'I saw some graffiti written on the back of a toilet door that said *"I fucked your mother"*, which is not that clever as far as graffiti goes, but underneath that, in different handwriting, someone had written, *"Dad, you're drunk, go home!"'*

This joke got nothing for Wil, so he tried his second joke. 'I bought a glass biscuit jar the other day and it came with instructions. Think about that. Instructions! I'm sorry, but if you need instructions to open a jar, I don't think you should be trusted with glass.' This got a small titter, so he kept on with the third joke.

'On a can of deodorant there is a warning that says: *"Do not spray in eyes!"* Who has sweaty eyes? What moron wakes up in the morning and thinks, "Gee my eyes stink!"?'

He couldn't believe that these jokes didn't get anything but, remembering what the emcee had said, continued into his fourth joke, which he finally got a big laugh for. The gig ended up going so well that when he got to the end of his spot he thought, 'Bugger this, I am going to try those first three jokes again.' So he repeated them all and thought that they finally got the respect that they deserved.

Rod Quantock and Brad Oakes were once employed by the Australian Services Union to do some gigs on buses at 5 am, to Qantas employees who were on their way to work at Melbourne Airport. The union wanted to publicise that Qantas were trying to take the bus service away, so they logically thought that getting some comedians to try and make employees laugh at five in the morning would be a good idea.

Rod and Brad were given a megaphone each to use as amplification to tell their jokes, and every time Brad tried to turn the switch on, he would accidentally set the megaphone alarm off and an ear-splitting *whoop whoop* would fill the bus, and the ears of the poor employees. Not the best preparation for a comedy spot.

They said *what* ABOUT ME?

Reviews and criticism are part and parcel of being a performer – though sometimes it's not a nice part and the parcel is often on fire and filled with dog poo.

I remember the excitement of getting our first review for the Scaredies, which appeared in a local street press magazine. The review was written by a local 'journalist' who had gained a bit of a reputation for writing scathing reviews, often about people he knew. My, possibly naive, opinion of reviewers in general was that they were usually bitter people and were often failed performers, though since that time I have met some reviewers and they aren't all failed performers.

Regardless, our review said that we were 'family friendly' (which we were), 'innocent' (again guilty as charged) and 'scatological'. Which we agreed that we were after we looked up the word 'scatological' in the dictionary:

> *Characterised by obscenity or preoccupation with obscenity, esp. in the form of references to excrement.*

I always wondered about what type of family the reviewer came from if they thought that 'obscenity in the form of references to excrement' was 'family friendly', but, you know … whatever …

WHAT, AND GIVE UP SHOWBIZ?

You can talk to many comedians or actors, and I am pretty sure that they won't remember the name of any reviewer who gave them a glowing review, but they will have etched into their mind the name of anyone who has crossed them in print.

By the way, I am talking about pre-social media days here. Back in the days when the only option for reviewing a show was in print or on the radio, things were a bit different. Nowadays the internet has provided ways for gutless, nasty people to easily spread anonymous vitriol, usually through jealousy. At least the gutless, jealous vitriol that I spread in these pages has my name written on the front cover.

One of the worst reviews we got opened with, 'Nothing sinks the soul more than an unfunny comedy record.'

I still remember both the reviewer's name and the sinking, useless feeling those words gave me. Not that I am holding a grudge – I have got over it, and actually that song to which he was referring is really not that funny – but I did just look him up on Facebook and I have *waaay* more friends than he does, so get fucked R– P–.

Early on in their career, Lano and Woodley received the following review for their first-ever show in Adelaide:

> Lano and Woodley are a fine example of what Max Harris calls 'the sad history of Australian comedy'.
>
> In their Magpie Theatre Show called 'Fence' at the Lion Theatre, nothing much happens very slowly. It's all much ado about male bonding over the back fence.

THEY SAID *WHAT* ABOUT ME?

Lano and Woodley lack timing and halfway reasonable material. Their deconstructivist comedy has plenty of gags worth running away from.

'Fence' is almost offensive and is certainly a load of old rope.

Quite why these Melbourne comedians are being forced on to unsuspecting school students in the name of entertainment is beyond me.

It's common to take favourable parts of reviews then add some ellipses ... and put them on to a poster to make your act sound good. Let's see if we can do that to this review to give Lano and Woodley a few tasty quotes should they ever want to get back together.

Lano and Woodley's review in all its glory
(Colin Lane)

Lano and Woodley ... fine example ... of ... comedy.

... their ... timing ... is ... a load of ... entertainment.

Luckily for Frank and Col, I think that some of their later reviews were a bit better ... I ... think ...

Poor old reviewers, hey? Once upon a time each major newspaper in a city would have just one or two main reviewers – a theatre reviewer and a restaurant critic. They were the toast of the town and were sucked up to by producers, publicists and restaurateurs desperate for a favourable appraisal of their latest musical/lemon tart. Since the internet has become a part of our lives, the power has been somewhat taken away from these reviewers. Now if they want to receive a similar level of being-sucked-up-to, they have to have their own reality television show.

If a bad review was printed just once in a newspaper, it wasn't that hard to take because it was as good as gone by the next day, whereas online reviews are there pretty much forever. Before any of us make the commitment to buying a ticket to a comedy show, we can watch footage on YouTube, be sent hilarious Twitter updates, and read honest reviews by real people giving their opinions about the show, or at least read honest reviews by real employees of the producer with fake email addresses giving their opinions about the show.

So, it's goodbye to the old-style newspaper print reviewer and hello to any old fuckwit who wants to write a good or bad review of a show, as demonstrated by this story:

During a festival run in Melbourne one year, Greg Fleet received a call from his manager, who told him that there were a couple of nice reviews online about his latest show. Fleety looked them up and saw that they were, indeed, very complimentary, and the reviews were from the two main newspapers in Melbourne – *The Age* and the *Herald Sun* – so they were probably even written by real journalists.

After reading the reviews, Fleety was feeling pretty good about himself, thinking, 'Oh yeah, I rock!' Then he noticed that below one of the reviews, members of the public could add their own comments. There were three comments that had been added, and

Greg decided to give them a read. The first two were short and glowing assessments of the show. Greg was thinking that was four amazing reviews in a row, 'I am pretty marvellous!' Then he read the third review. He said he had read each of the previous reviews once each, but he has read the third comment about 40 times – so now he knows it off by heart. Here it is:

> *Rather than go through the pain of watching such trash, I would rather sit in a dentist's chair reading chapters from the Bible. This is the WORST live show I have ever seen anywhere. Shame on you Greg Fleet, you fucking hack. You are a disgrace to comedians everywhere. People of Melbourne, do yourself a favour and spend your $30 on a hand job. At least you will leave the room feeling good with a smile on your face.*

Mum, Dad, I'm gonna
BE A COMEDIAN

Before the Scared Weird Little Guys did our first tryout spot, John and I had performed at least a couple of hundred paid gigs together in other groups. I don't want to say professional gigs, because not all of them were, but they were for money, so even at that early stage of our careers, we were both reasonably experienced performers in terms of getting up in front of an audience. In the two groups that we were in before starting the Scaredies – first a barbershop quartet, then a five-part a capella group called the Phones, we even got some laughs for bits that were meant to be funny. But it wasn't until we did our first tryout spot at the Hilton Comedy Club in 1990 that we had specifically written all of the material to get laughs. And the very first time you get a laugh for a joke that you have written is a unique and special memory. Being a somewhat experienced performer didn't really make a difference to my nervousness that night, because doing comedy for the first time is unlike anything else.

Cut to 23 years and about four and a half thousand gigs later. I was standing side of stage at a local comedy gig on a cold Monday night, nervous as all hell, as I was about to do my first-ever solo comedy spot. In many respects I had been there before, but always with someone else by my side. I'd delivered plenty of routines onstage by myself during Scaredies shows, but always with that secure thought that my stage partner was not far away. I've also done plenty of emceeing and hosting trivia nights and school fetes by myself and been fine. But a solo comedy spot was

WHAT, AND GIVE UP **SHOWBIZ?**

The line-up of shows for the weekend of 20 July 1990 at Le Joke in Collingwood, Melbourne. The 'John and Rusty' spot was the second ever gig of the Scared Weird Little Guys – before we had decided on the name
(Stef Torok)

something I had never done, and I thought it was time I experienced it for myself. I reckon performing comedy is mostly self-confidence, plus a good whack of preparation. Throw in some half-decent material and that's about it, there you go. There's some free advice for anyone thinking about getting into showbiz.

So my solo spot went fine, and I gained some new respect for all of the poor saps in this book that get out there and stand alone on a stage, night after night, in the pursuit of making people laugh.

When you first start doing gigs, apart from having poorly developed bad gig radar, you're also ready to say yes to any gig, because you're happy to be getting anything. There are a few 'red light' words that usually set the bad gig alarm bells ringing, and by now you should be getting a pretty good idea of what those words are. Let's list them here.

'Bucks' night' is a fair warning sign. You should also be wary of any gig involving the words 'footy' or 'free comedy night'. Steer clear of any gig that involves the words 'happy' and 'hour', in that order. You don't really want an audience whose first inkling that there is about to be a comedy show is, 'Why is that bloke talking on a microphone? Hey, ten dollar jugs of beer!'

Tommy Little was doing a spot at a pub called the Exford in the city of Melbourne. I'm not saying it was rough, but at that time it was said that if you haven't had your vaccination shots, you shouldn't bother going there. One night before a comedy show, a bouncer was stabbed and the show still went on, accompanied by the sounds of ambulances arriving.

Tommy had only been doing comedy for a few months, and had about six gigs under his belt, when he scored the spot at the Exford. He had been learning much about comedy from fellow comedian Tom Siegert. This is the same Tom Siegert who we heard about in the story of the Koo Wee Rup footy incident with Dave Thornton. Tom was hosting that night at the Exford and he could see that it was going to be a fairly rough crowd. He also noticed that Tommy Little was getting very nervous, so he gave Tommy a valuable piece of advice for any comedian – get a 'saver joke'.

Tommy asked what he meant and Tom Siegert said, 'When a gig starts to go badly and things start to turn, you should have your best joke ready to go, and that's called your "saver joke". Don't play it too early, though, because when it's played right, it can save a gig that's turning nasty.'

It's a fine piece of advice for up-and-comers and experienced comedians alike. The young Tommy asked his new mentor, 'So, what's your saver joke?'

Tom replied with the 'My first car and my first sexual experience were both old escorts', which is a fine joke and is a perfect 'saver joke'.

Tommy thought for a while and made a mental note of one of his best jokes, and he was now the proud owner of his very own 'saver joke'.

When it was time for the show to start, Tom Siegert headed out onto the stage, grabbed the microphone and said cheerfully, 'Good evening, everybody, welcome to comedy at the Exford!'

Immediately a very large, very mean looking bloke at the bar yelled out, 'Fuck off, cunt!'

Tom was a bit stunned by that reaction and he looked over to the bar and looked back to the audience and said, 'My first car and my first sexual experience ...'

Celia Pacquola recalls that when she was eight years old, she slipped in another girl's vomit during a performance of the Australian Girls Choir. Celia didn't mention if she was actually a member of the Australian Girls Choir at the time, or if she was merely running across the stage during their performance, staging a protest at their arrangement of 'I am, you are, we are Australian'.

Celia also told me about the first time she ever had a heckler. She was performing as part of the Melbourne University Law Revue. She was neither studying law, nor attending Melbourne University; she was just a huge fan of *The Late Show* and knew that most of them had started out doing the Law Revue, so she thought that would be a good place to start her performing career. The first sketch she was in had her playing a dodgy Cockney character wearing a scarf and a hat, and she swears she has never tried to play any kind of character since then. She was onstage doing an accent she describes as being Julia Gillard doing Eliza Doolittle *before* she became a 'fair lady', but she was wearing a hat and a scarf, which apparently made it believable.

She delivered her big line in a struggling Cockney accent, which was, 'Although I've never actually left my house, I do know the sound of every bird.' No one laughed, although when you read that line out of context, I think it sounds quite amusing. During the silence that greeted Celia's punchline, someone in the crowd burped, which got a far bigger laugh than anything that had been in the show up to that point.

Brisbane boy whose accent implies otherwise Josh Thomas had a strange gig early in his career, where he was booked to host a 'whole prawn wonton eating contest' at a Melbourne shopping centre. After the excitement of the competition was over, and the first prize of a year's supply of whole prawn wontons was awarded, the company refused to pay Josh his fee. This was obviously a problem for Josh, as volunteering to host 'whole prawn wonton eating contests' was not really a habit of his. He understandably maintained that he hosted 'whole prawn wonton eating competitions' in shopping centres strictly for the cash.

The reason that the whole prawn wonton company refused to pay Josh for the gig was because they thought that he was 'a bit awkward'. Awkward is what Josh Thomas does better than most people. Saying that Josh is 'a bit awkward' is like saying Hitler was 'a bit racist' or that Kyle Sandilands is 'a bit of a cockhead'. So Josh found himself in a legal battle with a wonton company over awkwardness, which is something that not many people can make a claim to.

I've always thought that the audiences at weddings are among the best you can perform for. Everyone is happy, not just because of the good feelings they have for the bride and groom, but also because of the free food and booze. Many of the wedding guests know each other, and they always know at least the bride or groom, so there is plenty of room for in-jokes and jovial references to past relationships and escapades. I have seen some wedding speeches done by people who have never been on stage or written a joke in their lives which get massive laughs amid touching and heartfelt anecdotes. For a comedian to 'die' onstage at a wedding requires a special level of incompetence or inexperience. We will blame inexperience for this tale from amusing bearded bloke Harley Breen.

Harley had been doing stand-up gigs for a little under three months when his sister asked if he would be the emcee at her wedding. She was planning the wedding herself and even went to the extent of attending a couple of Harley's gigs so that she could choose the exact jokes that he was to perform at the wedding reception. With so many important decisions to be made to ensure that her big day was perfect, I guess that choosing the jokes was not an unusual request for the bride-to-be.

Decide on filling for vol au vents – tick.

Choose font for commemorative wine glass engraving – tick.

Select appropriate jokes from little brother's comedy routine – tick.

The wedding was going to be a fairly conventional affair, with both the bride and groom, and most of the guests, being enthusiastic Christians. At least seven ordained ministers, including the father of the bride, would be in attendance, as well as various conservative elderly relatives visiting from rural Queensland. Half a dozen state and federal politicians from various parties would also be there, including the former Labor shadow minister Cheryl Kernot, as the groom had worked for her for a few years.

The audience, which numbered around 150 people, was not exactly what you would describe as a seasoned comedy crowd. This didn't deter the fresh young comedian with nearly three months' experience under his belt. He launched into some of his jokes, which included this cracker:

'I was listening to a song the other day that went "You and me baby aren't nothing but mammals, so let's do it like they do on the Discovery Channel." Now, I've seen the Discovery Channel, and

I don't want to do it like that. Animals do some fucked up shit! For example, after the praying mantis has sex, the lady praying mantis bites the male's head off. Sure, I want my cock sucked, but not like that!'

I'm not necessarily saying that joke was inappropriate for that particular audience, but I think that we can all fairly assume that none of the ordained ministers were jotting it down to use in next Sunday's sermon.

Over the next few hours, Harley continued with his emcee duties, doing various jokes from his act, while bringing on the band and introducing the speeches.

While we're on the subject of weddings, what has happened to the old custom of reading out telegrams sent by friends and relatives who couldn't attend the reception? That tradition seems to have been replaced by the best man reading out text messages, and it just doesn't seem to have the same impact.

OMG! PLZ BIG LUV 2 U 2! IMHO U GUYZ ROK! ROFL!!!
CUL8R xoxoxoxo
Brytnee and Shayyne

Back to our friend Harley. His comedy was not going over well at all, but at least his sister and some of his immediate family were laughing at his jokes. During the silence that followed one punchline, he clearly heard one of his cousins laugh, and then saw another cousin hit her on the arm and snarl, 'Don't laugh, you'll only encourage him!'

With the official proceedings out of the way, Harley was approaching his big finale, but first he played a video that he and his brother had filmed earlier that morning. They had secretly arrived at each of the houses where the bride and groom were preparing for the wedding and filmed themselves sneaking in

Harley Breen around the time of his wedding MC debut (James Penlidis)

and crash tackling them to the ground and writing in permanent marker on their respective backs, 'Property of Jim' and 'Property of Alison'. The brothers thought it was hilarious but the video was met mostly with gasps and horrified looks from the wedding guests. Not one to be put off by audience members who were not only not laughing, but were openly discouraging each other from responding at all, Harley went ahead with the finale.

As mentioned previously, the bride and groom were practising Christians, and they had both happily maintained their virginity up until this point. For this reason, our young and inexperienced comedian, brother of the bride, thought it would be a hilarious tribute to the bridal party if he dressed up and lip-synched to Marvin Gaye's song 'Sexual Healing', complete with his brother dressed as a female backing singer. You'll possibly be relieved to hear that, no, he didn't decide to go with a black-face routine, though Harley said that may have actually gone over more positively with some of this crowd. Harley's brother, dressed as the back-up singer, spent most of the song trying to dry hump the groom.

It was less a tribute to the happy couple than a tribute to the Grand Final edition of *The Footy Show*.

Harley's sister and her husband remain happily married, and

now have a couple of kids. I am sure they all have a great laugh about the whole event whenever they catch up.

Jodie J Hill has worked as a radio presenter for many years, and like many people working in commercial radio, she cut her teeth as a stand-up comedian. She had been doing stand-up only for a few months when she received a call from a local booking agent asking if she would like to do a paid gig for $400 at a twenty-first birthday party in the outer suburbs of Adelaide – a little place called Elizabeth. A suburb with a name like Elizabeth sounds quite nice. It brings images to mind of lush green parks and gardens and streets filled with stately looking homes with crisply manicured hedges and spacious driveways. However, if the suburb of Elizabeth were to be given a more accurate woman's name, she might be named 'Shazza', and Shazza would be wearing jeans a few sizes too small, have a few teeth missing and be sporting a misspelled ankle tattoo.

Despite the potential for this to be a tough gig, Jodie was excited at the thought of the money. She dressed appropriately in hot pants and tails and set off for her first paying gig. She also thought she might be better off taking along a support crew, so she enlisted her tough-looking friend Melissa to make the one-hour drive with her. Melissa promised to tag along on the condition that she could drink Jodie's rider, and they had a lovely drive out to Elizabeth, but arrived late for the show after misreading the directions. They parked out the back of the large suburban pub and raced in to find her contact and get on with the show.

She met with the guy who had booked her, and I don't want to typecast his greased-down hair, open-necked shirt, medallions and tight pants by calling him a stereotypical name, so let's just call him Guido. Guido informed her that she was not part of a comedy show at all, but that she was expected to emcee an all-male strip show. The twenty-first birthday party had melded with a hen's night, and what better way to celebrate your coming of age than by looking at some oiled up, beefy bloke's cock and balls? This news was a bit of a surprise to Jodie, but she didn't want to let her trepidation show – she was a professional comedian now, after all.

Jodie started by doing ten minutes of material to the predominately female audience, which she described as a 'female comedian's wet dream' because much of her material focused on tampons and other girly stuff that blokes often don't think is funny. She had the audience raring to go as she introduced the first male stripper, who had the clever stripper name of 'Jack Hammer'. Jack came onstage and gyrated around for a while, eventually removing all of his clothes, until he was left with only a pink ribbon tied around his knob. This was quite a shock for the fresh-out-of-private-girls-school Jodie J Hill, who came on to continue the show and was so thrown by the enduring sight of Jack's 'hammer' with a ribbon on it that she completely forgot all of her material.

'Well ... okay ... wow ...' Jodie stuttered and paused, as Guido shouted at her from the side of the stage, 'What the fuck are you doing? Get on with it!'

She spluttered through a couple of half-remembered jokes before bringing on the next stripper, who was named 'Whip Wangsling'. While Whip was whipping out his whopping wang and winning over the whooping wenches with his wiggly one-eyed winker, Guido was briefing Jodie on the next stripper, who had the enviable title of 'Mr Nude Australia'. Before introducing Mr Nude, Jodie had to draw the winning raffle ticket to see which lucky audience member was going to get to eat peaches and cream with Mr Nude Australia – sorry – eat peaches and cream *off* Mr Nude Australia. Due to a stuff-up with the raffle, two different girls thought they held the winning ticket, and both of them charged up to the front of the stage and valiantly defended their right to the sticky, gooey prize. They started shouting and pushing each other as they saw their chance to slurp peaches and cream off a nude bloke's chest slipping away, as it were. Jodie had to step in and she only calmed the situation by promising that both of the girls could sup with Mr Nude Australia. She introduced him to the crowd and gasped at the size of his long mullet haircut as he started his writhing routine. After a minute or so he glared over at Jodie and snapped, 'Commentate! Commentate!' She was speechless and could only mumble, 'Well, folks, I don't know about you, but that's one of the biggest mullets I've ever seen.'

Mr Nude then lay down and poured a tin of peaches and a tub of cream over his chest while the two lucky ladies licked like their lives depended on it. While this was going on, the prone Mr Nude turned his head and shouted again to Jodie, 'Commentate! Commentate!'

Jodie said the first thing that came into her mind, which was, 'Oh my God, that's disgusting!' At which point one of the girls, accidentally or on purpose, bit Mr Nude on the chest, which caused him to sit up suddenly, knocking the two girls on their arses and sending peaches and cream in all directions, including a big creamy splotch on Jodie's hot pants.

At the end of the show, after all the strippers had finished, Jodie farewelled the happy and satisfied crowd and let out a sigh of relief. She had completed her first paid gig successfully, even though she had been running late and was thrown into hosting a strip show. She now only needed to pick up her cash and head home.

She headed backstage and found Guido standing among the strippers, who were busy de-oiling themselves, and asked him for her pay.

Jodie J Hill, obviously not affected by the sight of Whip's wang
(James Penlidis)

'Oh, we didn't get as many people in as we wanted, so I can only pay you half,' Guido tried.

Jodie was about to say, 'Oh, okay,' then thought, 'No! Fuck that!'

'Look,' she shouted in Guido's face, 'I came up here expecting to do a comedy spot for a twenty-first birthday party, and ended up introducing some moronic beefcakes doing oily dance routines!' she paused and looked at the strippers around her, 'Ah, no offence, guys'. They stared at her blankly. 'And I did a great job, too! Are you going to pay Whip Wangsling half his pay? What about Mr Nude Australia? I bet he's not working for half pay! I got peaches and cream spilled on my hot pants, for fuck's sake, and I am going to get paid the full amount!'

I bet Guido was not used to being talked to like this, especially from a girl in hot pants and tails. He stormed out of the room and returned a short while later with the full $400 in small notes and coins, which he dropped on the floor in front of Jodie and walked off. Jodie picked up the money and safely stowed it in her hot pants. On her way out of the pub, she saw Guido with some of his mates and calmly walked over to him and said, 'Thanks for having me,' and made him shake her hand, then said 'Goodbye!'

Two managers walk INTO A BAR

Having a manager is an essential part of the entertainment industry. I think. At least that's what my manager always told me. Here's a story that was told to me, not ironically, by my manager.

Two managers run into each other while walking down the street. The first one says, 'So, how's business?'

The other one says, 'Great, thanks. Actually I am on my way to see the latest comedian I have just signed. Do you want to come and check them out?'

'Sure thing,' says the first manager.

Half an hour later the two managers are standing up the back of a packed big city theatre. The comedian is on fire and the sold-out crowd is going crazy, screaming and shouting for more.

The first manager turns to the other and says, 'Wow, this guy is amazing! You've done so well!'

The other manager says, 'Yeah, but can you believe he's taking 80 per cent of my income!'

Ha ha, that's a nice little story usually told by artists who feel that giving up 20 per cent of everything they earn to someone who hasn't written the material or learned it or got up onstage doesn't sound like a fair deal.

Anyway, there are two things wrong with the above scenario. Firstly, the manager is probably taking more than 20 per cent and secondly, the manager would never actually go to watch a gig.

Living
THE DREAM

The Scaredies were often contacted by people asking permission to perform one of our songs. Most times it was just a group of teenagers wanting to do the song at a school camp or a scout concert and we would always say yes. Similar requests go to Tripod and Lano and Woodley for their material and, as long as you don't mind being sent a video of an 'interesting' re-interpretation of one of your old bits from a group of scouts around a campfire, the whole process is fairly harmless. Recently, one teenager fan came back to help Colin Lane in a curious way.

It's been quite a few years since Lano and Woodley have performed together and Colin likes to do the odd solo spot at a local comedy club to keep his comedy senses sharpened for the various emceeing and hosting gigs he gets. One night he decided to dust off an ancient routine from the Found Objects, the group that he and Frank had been in prior to starting Lano and Woodley. Col had always liked the routine, so he wanted to see if it could work as a solo bit, although some cynics believe he was really trying it out because he was too lazy to write new material. He got through it okay, but knew that something was not quite right with the ending. After he came offstage, another comedian, Dave Bloustien, approached him with the missing pieces of the punchline. Dave knew the routine off by heart, because when he was in high school he had performed it at a school concert and had never forgotten it. Dave was a little embarrassed, as he had never asked permission to do the routine, but at least Colin now knew that he couldn't pass the routine off as a brand new piece, which I am sure he never seriously tried to do . . .

A Melbourne comedian – for the purposes of this story let's call him Bob – once got a call from a venue owner to do a private function in three weeks time. He was going to get paid $200, which was pretty good money for the time. Two days before the gig, he got a call from the guy who booked him. For the purposes of this story, lets call him Fred. Fred said to Bob, sorry, but the gig was cancelled. Bob was a bit miffed at this news, as he had turned down a couple of other gigs that would have paid quite well, so he asked Fred for a cancellation fee. Bob wished that the laughter coming down the phone line had been for one of his jokes, given the raucous hilarity that was emanating from Fred's end of the phone.

Bob was feeling a little hard done by, so he dug his heels in and called Actors Equity for advice. Once the Actors Equity rep had stopped laughing, he advised Bob that he was legally entitled to a cancellation fee of the full amount. Bob called Fred and informed him of the conversation with Equity. This time Fred didn't laugh, and he started screaming at Bob down the phone, calling him all sorts of whatever. Bob said the more that Fred yelled at him, the calmer he felt and when Fred was done with the screaming, Bob said, 'I don't care what you say, you owe me $200 and I am going to get the full amount. I'm coming in tonight to pick it up.'

Bob went in to the venue that night and talked to the girl on the door who said, 'Look, Bob, I don't know anything about this at all, but I was told to give you this.'

She plonked down a large, heavy bank bag full of one-cent pieces. Bob couldn't believe it. He grabbed the bag and struggled back home with it. As well as being full of one-cent pieces, there was a two-page handwritten letter basically saying, in no uncertain terms, what Fred thought of Bob.

Bob had really needed that money, as he was going up to Sydney for the week, but he just dropped the bag of one-cent pieces in his hallway near the front door and forgot about it until he walked back into his house a week later. It was the first thing he saw, and the memories of the cancelled gig and the insulting letter flooded back to him. Bob stared at the bag of one-cent pieces for a minute then said to himself, 'Fuck it, I'm going to count it.'

So he sat down at his kitchen table with $200-worth of one-cent pieces and proceeded to count the entire amount.

Fred must have thought that Bob would never count it, as after the counting was finished, Bob discovered that there was only $164.95 in the bag. In one-cent pieces. Fred was a full 3505 one-cent pieces short.

Bob was fairly upset at all this, so he rang up Actors Equity again. When the Actors Equity rep had stopped laughing, Bob asked for them to pass on the following terms to Fred on behalf of Bob.

Bob wanted to be paid with cash or a cheque. He wanted Fred to confirm that this episode wouldn't affect the amount of work that Bob got from the Fred's venue (yeah, good luck with that) and he also wanted a phone call apology from Fred.

The next day Fred called up Bob to apologise and Bob said, 'Look before you go any further, I just want to go through that letter that you sent me.'

So they went through the letter, paragraph by paragraph, as Bob disputed the things that Fred had said, and at the end they agreed to make it all water under the bridge, but their relationship has never been the same. They are both still working in the industry.

WHAT, AND GIVE UP SHOWBIZ?

A group of comedians were playing a Sydney Leagues club in the early 1990s and came across some bikie-related fun. George Smilovici had been the first comedian to get up and had copped an onslaught from a group of large, bearded tattooed blokes not far from the stage. George gave as good as he got and through the course of their tete-a-tete, had established that one of the bikies had brought along his 18-year-old daughter, who was quite stunning and was standing alongside the group. Akmal was next on, though he had been backstage and was unaware of the bikies and the bikie offspring in attendance. At that time Akmal was doing a routine about the movie *Indecent Proposal*, the movie where a rich bloke offers Demi Moore a million dollars if she will spend the night with him instead of her new husband. Akmal's joke went along the lines of: 'Okay, so we've already established that Demi Moore is a slut, we're just negotiating on the price, right? But who here, if I offered them a million dollars, would have sex with me?' Akmal then focuses on a pretty woman in the audience for the next bit of his routine.

The other comedians, alerted by George, knew that this part of Akmal's routine was coming up, and they knew that if he targeted the bikie's daughter, all hell was going to break loose. They were all gathered in the wings just offstage, waiting to see what was going to happen. Of course Akmal spied the bikie's daughter and said, 'What about you down there? Yeah, you standing there next to that big tattooed thing. If I offered you a million dollars, would you fuck me?'

Then the bikie father yelled out, 'A million bucks! Mate, just buy her a fucken beer!'

Comedy superstar Dave Hughes had a tough time on his first trip to the Edinburgh Fringe Festival. His audiences were small and he received a few terrible reviews. He was not enjoying the shows and he couldn't even understand the hecklers. At the halfway point of his four-week season he was feeling a bit down and hoped things might turn around for him. While standing in a line at a bank, he overheard two girls talking about another stand-up show they had seen. They were bagging every aspect of the comedian from his accent to the poor quality of his jokes and, strangely, this actually made Dave feel better about his own experience – the thought that someone else may have been having a worse time than him. But that feeling didn't last long.

Dave Hughes around the time of his first career-boosting trip to Edinburgh
(James Penlidis)

As the line moved along and the two girls summed up their 'review' of the comedian that they disliked so much, one of them said, 'What was his name again?'

'I'll never forget it,' said the other, 'It was Dave Hughes.'

With over 3000 shows to compete with, it's notoriously difficult for acts at the Edinburgh Fringe Festival to attract audiences. However, when British duo Max and Ivan turned up to their venue one night, they found there was another reason for the small crowd. They received the news that their show had not sold many tickets due to the fact that a homeless man had taken a poo outside their venue, and therefore people were turned off going in and buy a ticket

During their final season at Melbourne's legendary Last Laugh, the Found Objects came to the part of their show where they chose a volunteer from the crowd. A middle-aged woman seated near the front was selected and she was helped up onto the stage by Frank. Usually an audience volunteer would be feeling a little taken aback when suddenly thrust under the bright stage lights to be facing an audience rather than sitting in one. To have been dragged up onstage and be facing the confident, anarchic members of the Found Objects must have been more than a little confronting for this woman, because as soon as she was escorted to the centre of the stage, she started slowly backing away from Frank, Col and Scott. On most stages it would be safe to do this, as you would be stopped by a solid wall at the back of the stage. However, the stage at the Last Laugh had quite an unconventional set up, in that it was multi-level and had at least four entrances to it from various doors, curtains and stairwells. It was down one of these stairwells that the hapless audience volunteer then fell. Backwards.

The audience gasped. The boys on stage looked at each other in horror and listened for any sounds of movement from backstage. Frank was the first one to spring into action, and he bounded through the curtain to the backstage area to retrieve the poor woman. He hoped she was uninjured and imagined he could triumphantly return her to the stage and continue with the routine, but when he got backstage she was nowhere to be seen. Frank called out, 'Er, hello?' but the only sound he heard was that of the nearby emergency exit door banging shut. The volunteer had decided to volunteer herself out of the building.

Frank headed back out onstage where the audience was

Frank Woodley, Colin Lane and Scott Casley performing as the Found Objects, as Frank realises he may have committed manslaughter
(James Penlidis)

expectantly waiting for news on the wellbeing of their luckless colleague.

For possibly the first time in his performing life, Frank didn't know quite what to say.

'Um, everything's fine,' he said, 'no one was hurt and ... ah ... let's just get on with the show then, shall we?'

Colin and Scott looked at each other. The audience was quiet and were obviously wondering what the hell Frank had done with the unfortunate volunteer. As far as they knew, she had just fallen backwards down half a flight of stairs and was probably lying there injured and/or unconscious. Some may have been thinking that Frank had just finished her off so there could be no lawsuit.

Frank actually expected that the woman would soon reappear in the venue after having simply exited through the backstage door and walking around to the front entrance of the building.

But she didn't. Despite Frank's insistence that everything was okay, the audience remained a bit sceptical, and the response to the remainder of the Found Objects show was underwhelming, to say the least.

I think that you can never quite regain the trust of an audience who think you may have just committed manslaughter.

In the late 1980s, two Melbourne comedians, Tim Smith and Andrew Goodone, started performing a frozen chicken puppetry act called the Basters Theatre of Prague. To accomplish this interesting-sounding act of entertainment, they tied pieces of fishing line to the wings and legs of two frozen chickens and manipulated the meaty marionettes to act out stories. They would usually perform twisted fairytales while speaking in dodgy eastern European accents that somehow always ended up sounding like Scottish people doing poor German accents. Despite their accents being nothing to crow about, the Basters Theatre of Prague was a very funny act that never failed to have the audience cracking up.

Though the idea was first developed as a quick throwaway bit at the Dick Whittington Tavern one night, with repeated performances Tim and Andy actually got quite adept at giving those chickens a surprising range of emotions and animation. They developed a great rapport, both with the audience and with the chickens, and would egg each other on to the enjoyment of all. Of course the chickens weren't actually frozen by the time Tim and Andy used them onstage. They had to be thawed out to give them flexible movement, so sometimes before a show the sound of two hairdryers could be heard backstage as Tim and Andy frantically defrosted recently purchased chickens. Once thawed, the chickens would get easier (and funnier) to operate as the days went by, though Tim said there was a limit of about four days before the chickens just got too foul to keep using.

One night they were playing as part of a comedy night with the singlet-wearing Western Australian duo the Empty Pockets at the Phillip Island Boardriders Club.

The place was packed and Tim and Andy were halfway through their chicken routine. During the normal course of the act, no matter what fairytale they were retelling, at some point Tim would pluck up the courage to take a 'long march across Europe' and walk out into the audience. He would usually head straight to the table of any hecklers or noisy patrons, where he would 'walk' the defrosted, pongy poultry over people, sit it on their heads and generally take any chance to ruffle their feathers.

This particular night, the Basters Theatre of Prague was retelling the story of Little Red Riding Hood, and Tim was squeezing between chairs and patrons, through the crowded room on his way to 'Grandma's house'. When he reached the back of the room, he realised he needed to be back onstage to play the 'Grandma' to Andy's 'wolf'. Andy, being the wolf, was on the stage at the other side of the room, knocking on the door and shouting something like, 'Och! Vair ist zat stupid old woman?'

So Tim had to hightail it through the audience to get back to the stage. When he was about halfway there, he felt someone grab hold of his arm and he thought, 'Oh come on, mate, I'm just trying to get back to the stage.' He gave his arm a good old yank to break free and continued back onto the stage. Once there, he started back into the routine, doing the tasteful 'chicken grandma riding on the bedpost' bit, when he noticed that Andy wasn't saying anything. His jaw had dropped and he was just staring

WHAT, AND GIVE UP SHOWBIZ?

Andrew Goodone and Tim Smith as the Basters
Theatre of Prague in happier times
(Andrew Goodone)

at Tim's arm with his eyes wide open. Tim could hear gasps of shock coming from the audience. He thought, 'What the hell is going on?' and looked down at his sleeve.

Tim was wearing a standard suit jacket that had three buttons at the wrist, and firmly entwined in the three buttons was a long, blonde lock of hair. It wasn't just a few strands of hair we're talking about here, Andy described it as 'half a ponytail' of hair – and at one end of the clump of hair an inch-long section of scalp was still attached! Tim looked at the hair then looked at Andy and Andy looked at Tim and they both went, 'Aaaaarrrggghhh!' The audience was having the same reaction as you probably are reading this, and the same reaction that I had when I first heard it.

The show must go on, of course, so Tim hatched an idea, untangled the clump of hair from his jacket and placed it on the top of his chicken. This made the chicken look uncannily like Fabio. They finished up the show, and I reckon that it was probably the first time that the story of Little Red Riding Hood had been told featuring a Fabio chicken wearing a human hair wig with flesh attachment. After the show Tim went to apologise to the woman, who now had quite a bit less hair than she had before the show started, and she was fine about it, if a little excited, saying, 'Wow, I'm like famous now!'

So, Tim came away from the whole experience with hair on his sleeve but no egg on his face, and a reminder that showbiz isn't always all it's cracked up to be.

Julia Morris has done her fair share of globe-hopping between Australia and Britain in search of the comedy dream. On one of her first trips to the UK she found herself onstage in Brixton one night with a crowd that she felt was being unusually quiet. She was about ten minutes into her act when someone in the audience said, 'Er, zip it up!'

Julia said, 'Zip it up? I've only got like two minutes to go.'

'No,' said the person in the crowd, 'zip up your trousers.'

'Uh oh ...' thought Julia, as she remembered that she was wearing a new pair of groovy ski pants with no underwear, and realised she had been displaying a 'small window into her hair' as she described it.

She said, 'Why didn't someone tell me? Why have you let me stand up here for the last ten minutes?'

Someone in the front row said, 'We thought you were doing it on purpose – because you're Australian.'

'Yeah sure,' said Julia, 'because of course in Australia we think that the best way to make a good impression when you go overseas is to say, "Hi everyone, I hope you enjoy the show today and by the way, here's my beaver!"'

Georgina McEncroe was in the middle of a Comedy Festival show in a smallish room and was being increasingly distracted by the crinkling sound of lolly papers being unwrapped by someone a few rows from the front. She could make out the form of a woman through the blinding stage lights and thought she'd try out a bit of cutting-edge audience member put-down by saying, 'Oh come on, lady, that's very distracting. Unless you're going to share those with the rest of the class could you keep it down, please?' That, plus a few other smart comments got no reaction from the woman, until her male partner, who was sitting next to her, spoke on her behalf, which made Georgina go for the obvious comedian's response of, 'Oh, what are you, her spokesperson? What's the matter with her? She's got a mouth full of lollies and she can't talk for herself?'

The man said, 'Actually no, she can't talk because she is in the middle of a diabetic coma.'

Oh...

The Rhino Room in Adelaide was pumping on a busy Saturday night. There was a long line of punters outside the venue, patiently waiting their turn to file upstairs for the sold-out show. The bloke on the door, Tim, was busy taking tickets and directing the audience members into the venue. Two of the comedians who were on the bill that night, Adam Richard and Corrine Grant, were standing outside chatting and checking out the crowd when their attention was drawn to the very loud rumbling of 12 Harley Davidsons carrying leather-clad bikies pulling off Frome Street and entering the car park adjacent to the Rhino Room.

As the bikies dismounted and took off their helmets, Corrine laughed and said to Adam, 'How fucked would we be if those guys were coming in here tonight? You're a poof and I'm a girl, we'd be screwed!' She knew that they wouldn't be coming in though, as the room was sold out and all the punters were either already in the venue or lined up outside waiting to get in. That didn't stop the bikies marching over, ignoring the line and approaching Tim at the entrance. Tim was thinking, 'Oh my God! How am I going to tell a dozen mean-looking bikies that it's sold out and I can't let them in?' The first bikie, possibly their leader, stopped in front of Tim and, without saying a word, reached into his jacket and produced a stack of slightly crumpled pieces of paper, which he thrust in front of Tim.

'Here's our tickets, mate,' said the bikie politely, 'we printed 'em out so we wouldn't have to line up. Fucken Ticketmaster!'

Tim didn't tell the bikies that printing out your tickets didn't really entitle you to cut to the front of the line, but he silently smiled and nodded as the bikies filed past him into the venue.

When the show started, Justin Hamilton, who was hosting the night, bounced out onto the stage as he had many times previously. This time, however, he immediately noticed that something was up. The lights were bright in his eyes and his first words were, 'Woah, what's going on out there tonight?'

If his eyes could have adjusted to the light, he would have possibly seen 120 people using only their eyes to direct his attention to the 12 bikies lined up along one wall. It didn't take long for Justin to notice them, but he got into his routine and after a few minutes the audience started to warm up and relax, until one of the larger bikies started heckling. Justin was shitting himself, but he knew he was going to have to take one for the team and try to stamp some authority early, or the comedians following him would have trouble for the rest of the night.

Justin pulled out one of his standard heckler lines: 'You better save your breath, mate, so you can blow up your girlfriend when you get home.'

There was an anticipatory hush from the crowd to see the reaction from the bikies – who then roared with laughter at their heckling compadre. This drew more laughs from the rest of the crowd and gave Justin more confidence to continue.

'If I wanted to hear from an arsehole I would have farted.' Again this elicited a huge response from the rest of the bikies and the crowd, which possibly made Justin just a bit cocky when he said, 'Listen mate, I'm up here working. I don't come down and knock the sailors' dicks out of your mouth while you're trying to work, so shut up!'

This smashed the crowd, so he kept the vibe going by bringing on the first act, then he exited through the curtain at the rear of the stage. Justin exhaled, feeling pretty good about himself, then he heard a gruff voice say, 'You!' He turned around to see that two of the bikies had jumped onto the stage and followed him through the curtain and into the backstage area. One was a big bikie, and the other was a bigger bikie. The big one said again, 'You!'

Justin looked around in the hope that the big bikie was talking to someone else, but he was alone, and he swears that a small bit of wee may have come out. Before he could say a) sorry, or b) his prayers, the larger of the two bikies placed both of his enormous, tattooed hands on Justin's shoulders, looked him straight in the eye and said, 'Mate, the way you laid into Colin out there was fucking spectacular! You're a little legend! Do you drink Bundy and Coke?'

'Ah, yes,' said Justin, even though he didn't.

For the rest of the night, whenever he got offstage, a large bikie would appear seemingly from nowhere and place a Bundy and Coke in Justin's hand.

The weirdest thing to come out of that night is not that Justin met a bikie named Colin, but that now, whenever he has a Bundy and Coke, a bit of wee comes out.

For Josh Thomas, the rise from playing spots in comedy clubs to headlining your own show in larger theatres came quite quickly. He says that making that jump in a short space of time was a difficult thing to do in terms of his performance, and that it even added to his 'awkward' stage persona. One thing he had to get used to was being asked for autographs and being recognised on the street, so he decided to do signings after the show and sell posters, with the proceeds going to charity. He had trouble deciding which charity the money should go to as, let's face it, pretty much all charities are worthy, so Josh decided to let the audience decide. In retrospect, it was not such a good idea.

The next night at the end of the show he was explaining his plan to sell the posters for charity and asked a packed audience, 'What charity do you think I should donate the money to?'

There followed a barrage of people shouting out what seemed like everything that is wrong with the world today:

'Leukemia!'

'Canteen!'

'Epilepsy Foundation!'

'The AIDS Council!'

'Alzheimer's Australia!'

Canteen, the charity for young people living with cancer,

was the first one that Josh had heard through the cacophony of diseases and human misery, and he decided that it was a very worthy cause, so he said to the audience, 'Okay, let's choose Canteen for tonight.'

Most of the crowd of course agreed with Josh that Canteen is a very valid cause, but then a woman from near the back yelled out, 'Muscular Dystrophy Association!'

Josh said, 'Look, I'm sorry but I've already decided upon Canteen for tonight and I don't think I can just change that now.'

'Muscular Dystrophy Association!' shouted the woman again.

'Again, I'm sorry,' said Josh, now realising that this had been a bad idea, 'But I'm going to go with Canteen because it was the first one I heard.'

'Canteen is just a shorter name than Muscular Dystrophy Association, and that's unfair because it's quicker to say,' she shouted back.

'Well maybe the Muscular Dystrophy Association should have thought of that when they were deciding on a name,' replied Josh.

'My son has muscular dystrophy and he's here, sitting beside me,' said the woman.

Josh had no choice but to then say, 'All right then, from now on the money from the posters is going to the Muscular Dystrophy Association.'

The next night, instead of asking the audience for a charity, Josh told that story we have just heard and said that the money would be going to the Muscular Dystrophy Association, when a woman softly called out, 'Ah, Josh, tonight could you give it to spina bifida? Because I've got spina bifida.'

From that point onwards, at the end of each show Josh now simply says 'proceeds will be going to charity'.

LIVING THE DREAM

Dave O'Neil was on the job one night, living the dream for a sixtieth birthday gig at a winery up in the hills of Warrandyte, Melbourne.

The birthday boy's attractive and much younger wife, Jane, had organised the gig and she wanted Dave to be a surprise, but when he arrived at the venue there was nowhere for him to hang around that was out of sight, so she seated him at one of the tables with some of the guests, telling him that if anyone asked, he would just have to pretend to be someone who knew the guest of honour. The crowd of about 50 people consisted mostly of old school friends and people from the birthday boy's work, plus a few friends of Jane's.

Dave was sitting at the table adjacent to the birthday boy, who kept looking suspiciously over at him until he finally leaned over and said, 'So, who are you and why are you here?'

Dave, trying to keep the 'surprise' element happening said, 'Oh, I'm an old school friend of Jane's.'

The birthday boy instantly demanded, 'You used to go out with her, didn't you?'

'No, no, we're just old friends,' Dave said defensively, wondering why he was suddenly having to create a fictitious backstory, denying a relationship with the birthday boy's wife.

'So, what do you do then?' asked birthday man warily.

'Oh great,' thought Dave. Not only did he have to think up a fake relationship with the man's wife, but now he had to come up with a fake career. He panicked a bit and said the first thing that came into his mind.

'I run a farm around here,' he blurted, instantly regretting his decision, as Dave does not look like a farmer, and the closest he ever gets to farming is buying potatoes with the dirt still on them.

'What sort of farm?' asked the increasingly suspicious birthday boy.

Dave was already in over his head, so he thought he might as well run with it, and he said, 'Oh, it's an educational farm. I take school groups around and teach them about farming practices and other farming ... things ... '

'What type of farming practices?' asked birthday boy.

'Ahh, you know ... all of them ...' Dave was trying to remember any types of farming practices he had learned about at school, 'Organic farming, um, subsistence farming.'

'In Warrandyte?'

Thankfully, at this point Dave was saved by the birthday boy's wife, who called for the attention of the room as she introduced the special guest entertainer, who was, of course, Dave.

Dave stood up and said, 'Actually I am not a former school friend of Jane's, and you might be surprised to know that I am not a local farmer and indeed know nothing of the farming practices here in the Warrandyte area. I am Dave O'Neil.'

When there was no response to this revelation, Dave continued, 'Dave O'Neil the comedian.'

A polite smattering of applause greeted Dave as he launched into his routine, which largely centred around the birthday boy being a jealous old guy with a spunky younger wife.

Launching an attack on the guest of honour can often be the way to get to a tough crowd.

Lawrence Mooney was playing the Warrnambool Football Club's annual auction one year. The night featured over 120 separate items up for auction, so the crowd was completely exhausted by the time the entertainment started. Lawrence was brought on to the stage with an intro that went, 'Thank Christ that auction's over, now here's a comedian.'

He started doing his regular material but was getting nothing at all from the crowd, so he used the old favourite of going for the person in charge.

'Where's the senior coach?' he asked.

'He's gone home,' came the shouted reply.

'Thank God, because he looked like a fucking idiot in that shirt he was wearing.'

The whole room erupted with a loud cheer. Sometimes it's as simple as that, and Lawrence proceeded to just lay into the coach for the next 20 minutes. Lawrence said, 'I just basically called this guy everything under the sun and they lapped it up. I called him boring, stupid, questioned his intelligence and his sexuality.' In some situations, that is the only kind of stuff that the crowd will go for.

Other times it is best to leave the boss alone. Dave O'Neil had thought he had killed after one particular corporate gig where he had done some material about the CEO. Often in the briefing before one of these shows, there will be warnings from the organisers to not mention anything about certain people.

These warnings are often preceded with a standard phrase that reads the same no matter what type of gig it is:

'Last year the comedian/juggler/trivia night host offended the CEO/managing director/visiting dignitaries' religion/mother/trophy wife, so please steer clear of any references to politics/herpes/One Direction.'

Dave's gig was for a photo-developing company and he had obviously not received the standard warning letter, as he made reference to the age difference between the CEO and his much younger wife, as in, 'How did you meet? Is this one of those PE teacher/student things? Or are you actually the same age and it's just that working with all those photochemicals has aged you prematurely?' The rest of the crowd loved it but the next day his agent informed Dave that the CEO was very unhappy and would be docking his pay for doing the gig.

The warnings to stay away from certain topics are not just about individuals, either. A briefing for a mining company gig that the Scaredies did once said, 'Can you please not mention anything about the recent events where ten of our employees were murdered by terrorists in the Middle East?' Well, they could have told us earlier, I thought. After we'd spent all that time writing the hilarious 'Ten Dead Employees' Song ...

Bad news
TRAVELS FAST

On one tour around Canada, the Scaredies were criss-crossing the country at the same time as the improvisational group the 3 Canadians. We had made good friends with Eric, Derek and North on their many visits to Australia in the 1990s. Some said they were in Australia so often they should have changed their name to the 3 Canadian Australians. Others said, behind their backs, that they only spent so much time in Australia because they were unknown in their own country. Not me, of course, I wouldn't have said that. Not behind their backs anyway.

Anyway, thanks to us (some said), the 3 Canadians were now discovering the delights of touring regional community colleges in their own country. In most of the colleges the Scaredies were booked in, we would see posters around the place advertising upcoming 3 Canadians shows, or notice that they had recently done the same gig that we were about to do. If we were at a college before the Canadians, we would often leave a message for them in a sealed envelope to be opened before they did the gig. They would do the same for us, and that's why, as we were preparing to do our performance to 25 dullards in a fluoro-lit college cafeteria one night, we were handed an envelope addressed to the 'Square Queer Little Guys' by the organiser of the gig. This gig in Northern Ontario had seen us arrive after one of our agent's typical horror travel schedules. The night before, we had performed at some forgettable gig located an hour's drive out of St Louis, Missouri. That morning we had a 7am flight via Chicago to

WHAT, AND GIVE UP SHOWBIZ?

The 3 Canadians – yes, there are four of them and
thankfully they had better jokes than that
(James Penlidis)

Toronto, followed by a three-hour drive up to Owen Sound on the picturesque shores of Lake Huron. We were tired and cranky and nearing the end of a ten-week tour, so it was encouraging to receive a letter from our little Canadian buddies. I opened the envelope and there were two words written in a child-like scrawl...

SHIT GIG

Numerous people have contributed stories to this book, but many of them had trouble recalling some of their tales of bad gigs until their memories were jogged, usually by other performers. Comedians seem to remember bad gigs by other comedians more than their own bad gigs. It reminds me of the old joke:

First comedian: 'Did you hear that Joe Bloggs did a two-week sell-out season at the Sydney Opera House and scored his own television show?'

Second comedian: 'No, I didn't hear about that.'

First comedian: 'Did you hear that he played the Wodonga RSL in front of 12 people and died?'

Second comedian: 'Oh yeah, I heard about that!'

The masters of the vocal gunshot and door slam, the Umbilical Brothers, took a chance in 1999, relocating to New York City for 12 months to have a crack at doing their rubbery limbed mime and punching noises in an off-off-Broadway theatre. After a few months of struggling for audiences, they hooked up with a producer who got them some national television appearances, plus a spot at the infamous music festival Woodstock 99, in upstate New York.

They were flown up in a helicopter, and as they approached the festival site they witnessed the incredible scene of a few hundred thousand people trying to have fun at a disused, treeless air base in 40-degree-Celsius heat. David and Shane were overwhelmed at the scale of the gig as they were shown through the seemingly endless backstage area on their way to the first of two gigs they were to play that day – on the main stage in front of 100,000 people. David read out to Shane the running order of some of the bands that would be appearing:

Red Hot Chili Peppers

The Offspring

Counting Crows

Limp Bizkit

Rage Against the Machine

Metallica

'Our subtle brand of theatre-based mime and sound effects should fit right in,' he said, getting a bit worried and wondering just what the hell they were going to do in front of such a huge festival crowd.

As they were taken to the side of the stage, they got to see a bit of the artist that they would be following – a little act called James Brown. The godfather of Soul. You may have heard of him. Following James Brown? Sure, the Scaredies once had to go on after James Mathison, and that was tough – but James Brown!

Shane quickly came up with the idea that they should go out onstage pretending to be drug inspectors and freak the crowd out a bit.

They went on and said, 'Ladies and gentlemen, we are the official Woodstock drug inspectors.'

(Sound of a hundred thousand people booing.)

'Is there anybody here on drugs?'

(Sound of a hundred thousand people cheering.)

Shane started changing his voice. 'We have reason to believe that you maaaayyyy bbbeeeeeee expeeeeeeriencing-some-changes-in-your-perception.' They made things go faster, slower, put fake echo on their voices, made dogs appear out of nowhere and, as you can imagine, they killed. Sure, James Brown was good, but could he make an exploding dog appear out of nowhere?

After a quick backstage interview with MTV, who were showing pay-per-view coverage of the Woodstock Festival that year, the Umbies were rushed over to one of the smaller side stages to perform another longer set, again in between bands.

They arrived backstage to see a noisy metal core band called Spitfire onstage, rocking the crowd into a bouncing, sweaty, crowd surfing mass of youth and empty water bottles.

Shane and David assessed their options as to what bits of their routine they should do for this spot. Should they do the same drug inspector bit that had just killed on the main stage? Or should they do their 'Sorry, Mate' routine from the theatre show, which begins with half a minute of extremely quiet footstep sound effects and subtle mime?

The adrenaline rush of the previous successful performance had obviously given them an inflated perception of their own theatrical capabilities, as they were soon brought plummeting back to earth.

The metal core band finished with an ear-splitting distorted guitar and drum crescendo followed by a huge cheer from the crowd of about 3000 people. An uninterested-sounding stage manager then said into a microphone, 'Okay, guys, here's the Umbilical Brothers,' at which point Shane walked silently onto the stage and began the footstep sound effects that eventually lead to David walking onstage.

After about five seconds someone yelled out, 'What the fuck is this shit?' followed by, 'You suck!'

The calling out was relentless, as more of the confused, hot and amped up audience joined in on the fun.

'Fuck off!'

'Get the fuck off the stage!'

And, repeatedly, 'You suck!'

As a performer, one thing that surely cuts you to the core and makes you question your existence and value as a creative human is someone aggressively yelling 'You suck!' into your face while you are trying to mime on a large outdoor stage in front of a few thousand people.

The boys came off feeling dejected and embarrassed, a million miles away from the elated bullet-proof glow that they had experienced only 20 minutes previously. Showbiz can be one cruel son of a bitch.

They were back in New York City that afternoon, and the feelings of gloom were starting to disappear when they got to the theatre for the evening's performance and were told by the stage manager, 'Ahh, did you guys know that one of your performances was shown on MTV today?'

WHAT, AND GIVE UP SHOWBIZ?

David froze when he heard those words, hoping that MTV had broadcast the first spot on the main stage.

'Yeah ... wow,' said the stage manager, 'You could hear the people shouting out "You suck" really clearly ...'

Anthony 'Lehmo' Lehman was booked to perform at the Falls Festival in Lorne on the beautiful, rugged coast of south-western Victoria. The Falls Festival is predominantly a music festival, but to mix things up a bit and help the youthful punters maintain their interest across the four days of the event, there is a smaller stage set up in a tent that is an alternative to the larger, louder stage. In this tent, which fits about a thousand people, you can see a variety of acoustic acts, cabaret and circus acts, DJs, the odd noisy band, and stand-up comedy.

The crowd at the Falls Festival are mostly young Generation Y folks who are happy to camp out without washing, or eating well, or exhibiting many signs of being functioning human beings for three or four days. But in one respect they are very organised – apart from working out ingenious ways to smuggle alcohol into the festival site (hidden inside hollowed-out loaves of bread, apparently) – and that is working out when their favourite bands are scheduled to be playing, on which particular stage, then converting the information into a spreadsheet that they can follow across the whole festival to maximise their enjoyment. If one of the stages gets behind time, which is not out of the question at something so logistically difficult to coordinate as a large music festival, it will throw out the carefully planned spreadsheet, and if there's one thing you don't want it's a hot, hungry, dirty member of Gen Y with an unsynchronised spreadsheet of their favourite bands.

Lehmo was scheduled to play during the middle of the afternoon in the hot and steamy tent, as the third of the three comedians that made up the comedy element of that day's program. He was looking forward to the gig, because if there's one thing that works well in a muggy and crowded tent in the middle of the bush on a searing summer afternoon, it's comedy – said nobody, ever. Add to this the fact that by 3 pm the stage was already running 45 minutes late, so the crowd who wanted to watch the comedy had been and gone, and the crowd that was turning up for the act that was scheduled to follow the comedy had arrived, were confused and were getting the first inkling that their precious spreadsheets were starting to become irrelevant.

The programming of the afternoon could also have been a little more comedy-friendly, as the first two comedians went on, then a band played, then Lehmo was due to do his set directly before the Swedish electro indie-pop singer, Lykke Li (pronounced Lykke Li).

The emcee, Danny McGinlay, went out to introduce Lehmo and immediately got pelted with empty beer cans and clumps of grass, and I'm not talking about the fun kind of grass that you would usually find in abundance at these festivals. Danny gave Lehmo the most difficult intro you could hope for, along the lines of, 'Okay, guys, coming up we have Lykke Li!' at which the crowd went wild, then Danny continued, 'but first we have some comedy, please welcome Lehmo!'

Lehmo walked onstage to a chorus of boos and shouts of 'Fuck off!' and 'We want Lykke!'

It wasn't exactly like Lykke was ready to go on either, because one of the reasons behind having the comedians on at all was so the roadies could set up the stage for the next band. Nothing like trying to do jokes in a dusty sauna to a crowd that hates you, while a guy with his bum crack showing is setting up a drum kit, tuning guitars and shouting, 'Check waan, two ... wan, two,' into a microphone next to you.

It's a credit to Lehmo's self confidence/stupidity that in the first minute of his set, amid a shower of beer cans and abuse, he thought to himself, 'I reckon I can win these bastards over.' There actually was some laughter, but it was coming from the other comedians, who were watching the slaughter from the side of the stage.

The turning point for Lehmo came about five minutes into his 15-minute set, when he was hit in the ribs with a full beer can. His first thought being, 'Wow, that hurt!' and his second thought being, 'Wow, they must *really* hate me!' because he knew that the queue to buy beer tickets was two hours long, and the cost of a beer would have been about two hours' wages working at Subway, so these young ingrates were certainly committed to their cause of getting Lehmo offstage. That's when Lehmo thought, 'Fuck you,' and became determined to finish his 15 minutes. He paused and leant on the microphone stand as another full beer can whizzed by his ear, and casually said, 'Sooo, what else is going on?'

Chants of 'Fuck off wanker, fuck off wanker,' started up in random pockets of the crowd, and soon most of the audience joined in. At first this impressed Lehmo, then it alarmed him, as it meant that this crowd was learning and becoming more organised in their dislike.

After about 12 minutes, he decided to put everyone, including himself, out of their misery, and said, 'Look, I don't want to break any hearts, but I'm gonna go now.' This was met with a huge cheer. 'No hard feelings though, I understand this is a music festival and the stage is running late and I genuinely hope you all have a great time for the rest of the festival. Except for that bloke who hit me with the full beer can, I hope you choke on your own vomit and die!'

This gave Lehmo his biggest laugh of the gig and he left the stage, followed by a few flying cans, just in case he had any second thoughts. Ironically, Lehmo said that before the show he had been wandering around the festival site and running into a few friends and he told another comedian that he had a good feeling about the gig. So much for experience giving you radar about a bad gig. He also says that given the number of people who still come up to him and say, 'I was there at that shit gig you did at the Falls Festival,' there must have been at least 30,000 people in the tent that day.

Life on the ROAD

When the Scaredies were on one of our many driving tours around the southern states of the USA, we would mostly have our accommodation booked for us. Occasionally there would be the odd night between gigs when we would have to find our own place to stay. This offered a chance to do some exploring on the back roads, or do some actual sightseeing in one of the many famous towns in that part of the world.

The search for a motel in Memphis late one afternoon found us driving around a rather dodgy area of town, but how were we to know? This was before the internet and online travel blogs that could warn unsuspecting tourists which parts of a city might be potentially unsafe. We simply had a map and were driving from one point to another, which sometimes added to the fun, I guess. We spied an interesting-looking motel called the Hop On Inn or something like that. I got out of the car and approached the reception, which was just a small glass window, possibly bullet-proof. Seated behind this window was an overweight guy in a stained singlet, chomping on an unlit cigar.

'You have any rooms available, mate?' I asked.

'How many hours you want?' he drawled.

'Ah ...' I was a bit thrown, '... let me go and check.'

I walked back to the car.

'They're full. Let's go.' I said.

We found a nicer motel up the road a bit, checked in and spent a mostly incident-free night there. The only trouble I experienced involved a six-pack of Miller and a large bag of pork rinds. As we were leaving town the next morning, we drove back past the Hop On Inn and there was quite a scene happening. There were three police cars pulled up at the entrance and a police officer was putting crime scene tape over one of the motel room doors while another took photographs. The only thing missing was the chalk outline of a body. Two things went through my mind – 'That could have been me,' and, 'I wonder how many hours they paid for?'

Josh Thomas and Greg Fleet were doing some dates together in Ireland. About halfway through the run the club owner, Sean, came up to Josh about ten minutes before the show was due to start and asked him if he knew where Greg was. Greg has maintained a well-known, off-and-on heroin addiction for the past 20 years, so Sean asked Josh, 'Do ya know where Fleety is? You don't think he's had an overdose do you?'

Josh said, 'Oh no, definitely not. He's off drugs at the moment and I have been hanging out with him for the past few weeks and I swear he is fine. I'm sure he'll be along any moment now.'

Sean went off to the hotel where they were staying, in search of Greg. Fleety had been at the hotel in the afternoon and was feeling pretty good about life in general. He had been clean for over six months and was touring around Ireland with Josh, having a great time. Greg had been in the hotel bar since lunchtime, drinking Guinness with an Irish comedian friend. Fleety describes certain danger times in the life of a recovering addict, and this was one of those times. Having not taken any drugs for a while and being drunk, he started thinking, 'Ah yeah, I'm going great and I'm in control – maybe I could have just a little hit, I'll be fine, I'm sure I'll be fine.' He didn't take much convincing, so he went out for a little walk and, surprise surprise, he found himself in the 'wrong part of town', but the 'right part of town' for what Fleety was looking for. It didn't take him long to meet up with a guy who had some heroin, and Greg took him back to his hotel room. Five-star hotels apparently just love it when you bring homeless drug dealers back to your room, and a young hotel clerk made a mental note as they walked through the foyer – a deed which later probably saved Greg's life.

Greg had purchased heroin for himself and his new dealer friend, and as the dealer was shooting up he said, 'It's a bit shit so you should have a lot.'

Always one to do as he was told, especially when it's a homeless drug addict giving the advice, Fleety took note of the instructions, and the last thing he remembers was standing in front of the mirror in his hotel room, shooting heroin.

Greg woke up a few hours later in hospital, lying on a gurney and surrounded by medical staff. He remembers thinking, 'Why is everyone Irish? Why am I lying down and in a hospital?' It took a few more minutes before he realised that he must have overdosed, something he had never done over the past 20 years. His mind started to clear and he sat up and said, 'Fuck, I better get to that gig!'

Greg started getting dressed and preparing to leave the hospital, against the advice of the people looking after him. He jumped in a cab and went straight to the venue.

'I walked into the club, and the show had finished hours before. I found the club owner, Sean, and just went into that standard junkie thing of lying.'

Greg put on his best junkie lying voice and said to him, 'Oh sorry, mate, I was on my way here and these four guys jumped me and tried to rob me and I fought two of them off, then one of

From left: Anthony Morgan, Peter Rowsthorn, Greg Fleet and Andrew Goodone in the late 1980s
(Andrew Goodone)

them must have hit me with something and I've only just come to, and they took my wallet.'

Sean stood and listened to him with a deadpan look on his face, very slightly shaking his head, more out of pity than disbelief.

Greg was thinking, 'Uh oh, what's happening? This lying thing usually works for me ...'

Sean said, 'Listen, Greg, I went to your hotel, and thanks to the hotel clerk, we got into your room and found you overdosed on the floor. I put you into the ambulance and sent you off to the hospital.'

Fleety went, 'Yeah ... that's kind of what I meant when I was talking about getting here late ...' but it was far too late to be making excuses or continuing with the lies.

Sean gently said, 'Look Greg, I am a Christian …' and Fleety thought, 'Awesome! I'm going to get away with this!' But Fleety didn't know that there were very different kinds of Christians, and this Christian believed in a very angry God, and Sean proceeded to absolutely tear Fleety a new arsehole while giving him a complete and utter dressing down.

The next morning Fleety pondered the events of the previous day and thought, 'There are probably a few better ways to launch your international comedy career …'

The 3 Canadians spent a lot of time on the road and used to have some fun ways to amuse themselves. They were particular fans of the prank phone call, often performed just for the amusement of one or two of them while sitting in a hotel room. They also had a few stunts that they would pull in crowded public places, one of which I was lucky enough to experience first-hand. They would gather a group of friends together and head off to the movies, choosing the busiest session on a packed Friday or Saturday night. All of the group would head in to find their seats, except for Eric, the blond-haired nut who was also renowned for being arrested at a water park for sliding naked down a waterslide named 'Blue Streak' during a Christian Youth convention.

For their movie escapade, Eric would buy two buckets of the largest size popcorn available, then wait until the lights in the cinema were dimmed and the advertisements and movie trailers started playing. He would then enter the jam-packed cinema and start slowly walking up and down the aisles, pretending to search for his friends, while loudly whispering, 'Hey, guys! Where are you?'

It was guaranteed that, as Eric's pleas gradually grew louder and he slowly acquired focus, someone on the other side of the room would shout out, 'Over here!' Eric would then traipse down his aisle and head over to where the voice came from, all the while cleverly gathering more attention from the moviegoers. This charade continued over the next few minutes, with more and more people shouting out, 'Here we are!' and 'We're over here, mate!' with the unimpressed Eric, arms full of popcorn buckets, awkwardly running back and forth across the cinema, getting increasingly frustrated, appearing upset and shouting out, 'Shut up, you guys! I'm just trying to find my friends.' When he had gained the complete focus of the rowdy crowd, he would pretend to give up his search, shout, 'Oh, fuck you all then!' and run down the aisle to the very front row. Just as he reached the front and while silhouetted against the screen, he would then do a pratfall and throw both of the giant tubs of popcorn into the air, which would make the entire cinema erupt into an enormous shout of laughter and cheering.

Eric would then sit alone in the front row for the whole movie.

I just loved the commitment to pure fun those guys had. For Eric to put himself through all of that for the simple enjoyment of his mates and the general public was just brilliant.

One of the great things about touring is that sometimes you get to do it with other acts and share all of the experiences, good or bad.

Usually the gigs are at night, which leaves the daytime open for social activities. Tennis or games of golf are good if you are feeling active, as is catching an afternoon movie, which often involves judging if you have enough hours before show-time to fit in a sneaky joint to help pass the afternoon.

Sharing a meal is also a common occurrence that allows a bit of bonding and storytelling time.

A group of us found ourselves in Hobart with a rare night off and, with no show to prepare for, eight of us decided to head out for a slap-up lunch. We had a good friend who had recently moved down to the lovely Tasmanian city probably most famous for its circular casino and being the birthplace of *Baywatch* actor Jaason Simmons.

Our mate suggested we go to the Hobart Sailing Club as the food was recommended, we wouldn't need to make a reservation, and it had marvellous views of Hobart's handsome bridge that had collapsed back in the Seventies. We walked in around lunchtime and found that we were the only customers in the place. The room was L-shaped and the walls were covered with quaint black-and-white photos of sailing boats, along with old wooden honour boards filled with the gold lettered names of important past presidents and the even more important associate secretaries of the Hobart Sailing Club. It was charming and relaxing, and we looked forward to an enjoyable afternoon. We took a large circular table for eight at one end of the room, ordered some drinks and sat down. Someone produced a bag of hash cookies, which, after the obligatory, 'Hmm, I don't know … how strong are they?' questions, were broken into halves and eaten. After half an hour or so, things were cracking along quite nicely. The drinks and the banter were flowing freely, with much laughter and good times – until a hundred people walked through the door to attend a funeral.

The timing could not have been more perfect, if by perfect you mean that our meals, the sombre eulogies and the cookies all arrived simultaneously. The official funereal duties were taking place at the opposite end of the 'L' to our table, though there were so many people there that the crowd extended around the corner and some mourners were actually standing right next to our table. It was as ridiculous as it was surreal. One moment we had been laughing and joking around and the next we were listening to solemn stories about a dead sailor.

Some funerals can actually be a celebration of the life of the dead person, filled with glowing tributes and hilarious stories, but judging by the stories we heard that day, it seems that this bloke was not that popular and had actually been a bit of a bastard. His son said something like, 'Well, a lot of you know that I didn't really get on with dad that well, and I only came down here from Brisbane because my sister paid for my ticket.' I got the feeling that that was the *nicest* thing he could say.

So we all sat there, off our tits, eating our meals in silence. As we were on a circular table, we could only really look at each other, and because we were all extremely mature blokes in our late thirties, we were desperately fighting off the urge to burst into uncontrollable fits of giggling, but the seriousness of the occasion meant that we simply could not, under any circumstance, start laughing. Eight stoned men giggling , along with clowns and strippers, are just not what you want at a funeral, even if it is for an unpopular seaman.

The urge to laugh enveloped the table and threatened to burst all over us. I averted my eyes from the other idiots and dug a fork into my leg to try to repress the unrelenting need to snigger. Just before blood was drawn, I felt the self-harm approach starting to work and the uncontrollable urge abating. We were nearly ready to continue our excruciating meal in silence. That was until someone covered their mouth with a napkin and made a clearly audible fart noise.

Have you ever tried to suppress pure, uncontrollable laughter? Maybe in church, or while listening to a serious speech at school, or at a fucking funeral for someone you've never even met. I was slumped forward, my head down, my shoulders shaking and tears streaming from my eyes and dripping off my nose when one of the funeral-goers who was standing near our table leaned over and patted my back saying, 'Thank you so much for sharing in our grief. It really means a lot to us.'

Legendary Scottish comedian Stu Who? has had his fair share of interesting occurrences at gigs. He's been attacked onstage by a dwarf, had an asbestos safety curtain lowered on him as the audience aggressively rushed the stage, and had his genitals stroked mid-performance by a mental heckler. But I love this tale of a day of marathon travel to a gig that is peppered with bizarre incidents.

Stu's entertaining expedition began with a seven-hour train ride from Edinburgh down to Brighton, which is a long and tiresome travel day for anyone, especially if you have to perform a gig at the end of the journey. But Stu, being the hardworking humorist that he is, was well up for the challenge. He jumped on the train and grabbed a table seat, spread himself over two seats with iPod, magazines and inflatable pillow arranged appropriately, nicked off to the toilet to smoke a wee jazz cigarette, then settled down as the train lurched out of the station. Stu hoped to grab a nap along the way and with any luck wake up five hours later in London's King's Cross Station, the first stop on the journey to Brighton.

The train was soon swaying and rhythmically rocking along with the beat of the trance music in Stu's headphones, and his eyelids were getting heavy as his head was gently nodding along to the music, when he noticed that on the other side of the table, the elderly bloke sitting opposite him was also nodding his head to the beat, spasmodically, and in an increasingly agitated manner.

'Hmm, he's fairly loving this music too,' thought Stu. 'Wait a minute ... I'm listening on headphones, so how can he be hearing it?'

Then the twitching man's head dramatically dipped forward, landing on the table between them and remained there, unmoving.

The old bloke wasn't grooving along to the music with Stu at all, he was having a heart attack and the poor fellow actually died right there on Stu's magazines.

The train stopped at the next major station – Newcastle – and the relevant authorities came on board, interviewed the passengers and removed the man's body before the journey continued, now 90 minutes behind schedule.

Stu alighted – or is it de-trained? – at King's Cross Station and swiftly headed to use the station's toilet. As he entered a cubicle and sat down, a large, grubby hand appeared under the partition from the neighbouring stall.

'Gimme stuff,' said a deep, threatening and disembodied voice from the next cubicle.

'Fuck off!' replied Stu, sweetly.

'Gimme stuff, gimme stuff, gimme stuff,' repeated the voice.

Stu left the toilet but was followed by the grubby handed owner of the deep voice – a large, crazy looking bloke with a bung eye and a lingering odour.

The man followed Stu until he mercifully reached two policemen, just as he heard his train to Brighton being called for departure. He started to tell his story, then suddenly grubby hand was gone, so Stu nicked off to resume his increasingly strange trip.

He arrived in Brighton an hour before the gig, which was with the funny and famous lesbian comedian Rhona Cameron. Stu decided not to check in to his hotel as planned, but instead headed straight to the venue to meet the stage manager, whose name was Beverley.

He arrived and asked Beverley if he could do a sound check, as he had a musical backing track for an audience participation song that was part of his set. She looked a bit puzzled, but shrugged her shoulders and said, 'Sure, if you really think you need to.'

Stu wondered what she meant by that.

About 30 minutes before the show, Beverley the stage manager nervously shuffled into the dressing room and said, 'Uh, I have some good news and some bad news, which do you want to hear first?'

'I'll have the bad news, thanks,' said Stu, intrigued by her obvious nervousness.

'Well,' she said slowly, 'you know how this gig is part of the Brighton Festival's Minority Group Support Initiative?'

'No, I never knew that,' said Stu tentatively, and getting just a tad apprehensive.

'Well, it's a special show for minorities, and most of the audience are from the local Association for Deaf People.'

'Deaf people?' Stu asked. 'A deaf comedy audience?'

'Yes, but there's another problem,' said Beverley.

'That's not the problem? The fact that they're deaf?' exclaimed Stu.

'Well it is ... and it isn't,' said Beverley.

'Well that's good ... and that's bad,' said Stu.

'The problem is that the lady who was coming along to sign for the deaf has taken ill, so now we have no one to sign the show.'

'Really?' said Stu. 'You're telling me that we've got a deaf crowd and no signer? So, what's the good news?'

'Well, I have just been told that there is also a full busload of lesbians who are coming to see Rhona.'

'And how is that the good news?' asked Stu.

'Well, they're not deaf,' offered Beverley.

As show-time approached, Rhona arrived and blew a proverbial gasket at the impending doom-laden prospect of a predominantly deaf audience, with no signer, although that news was possibly tempered by the prospect of a busload of fellow lesbians to connect with. Interesting match of words that – 'fellow' and 'lesbians'.

Rhona and Stu then became hopeful when Beverley came backstage and said, 'I've got some good news!'

She informed them that she had found one audience member who was, in fact, a skilled signer who was willing to step into the breach and sign the show for them.

Stu felt relieved.

'But ...' Beverley continued.

'And here's the bad news,' thought Stu.

Beverley went on to tell them that the signer was painfully shy and couldn't face being onstage, so she would sit in a chair in the front row, listen to what was said, turn around to face the crowd without standing up and sign what had been said, then repeat the process, line by line and gag by gag.

And that's exactly what the woman did for Stu's entire half-hour set – including the song, whose sing-along chorus was participated in with gusto by the deaf majority audience, though, somewhat ironically, not by the busload of lesbians, who mostly sat silently and suspiciously through Stu's song.

As Stu lay in his hotel bed later that night, pondering what a long day of death, madness, deafness and gay abandon he had faced, he surely must have been thinking, 'What, and give up showbiz?'

EPILOGUE

'What's the worst gig you ever did?' is a very common question in interviews.

No one ever asks, 'Can you tell us about the best gig you ever did?' Stories about failure, embarrassment, humiliation and disaster are so much more fun than one that goes, 'Well, there were a thousand people in the audience and they all paid full price. No one was late, the sound system worked perfectly and the lighting was functional. I remembered all of my material, I didn't fall off the stage and the show started and finished on time. There were no hecklers, my pants stayed up and I got paid the full fee in hundred dollar notes, before the show. No one lost any of their scalp, nobody got stabbed and no one overdosed. There were no sailors, prisoners, soldiers, footy players, lions, snakes, bats, children, vomit, strippers, bucks' nights or bikies. My intro was concise and accurate and I got a five star review.'

What, and give up showbiz?

Why the hell would I ever want to give up showbiz?

ACKNOWLEDGEMENTS

I am very grateful to all of the wonderful performers who so generously shared their stories in this book. Here is a list of them, in alphabetical order:

Akmal, Wil Anderson, Dave Bloustien, Harley Breen, Dave Callan, Damian Callinan, Doug Chappel, Tommy Dean, Marty Fields, Greg Fleet, Russell Gilbert, Andrew Goodone, Corinne Grant, Justin Hamilton, Jodie J Hill, John Fleming, Adam Hills, Dave Hughes, Colin Lane, Lehmo, Tommy Little, Trevor Marmalade, Georgina McEncroe, Lawrence Mooney, Julia Morris, Simon Munnery, Brian Nankervis, Brad Oakes, Dave O'Neil, Celia Pacquola, Rod Quantock, Glenn Robbins, Denise Scott, George Smilovici, Tim Smith, Greg Sullivan, Josh Thomas, Dave Thornton, Tripod, Umbilical Brothers, Stu Who? and Frank Woodley.

There are so many more people that I would have loved to have included in this book but couldn't for a number of reasons, time being the most obvious. Plus, some comedians insisted, of course, that they had never had a bad gig, or at least 'couldn't remember any'. Also, trying to organise to meet up with three or four comedians at a certain time on a certain day can be surprisingly and frustratingly difficult for people who do nothing during the day.

Huge thanks and love go to my family. My loving and patient wife Denise, and my beautiful children Hank and Mary-Lou, who surely grew tired of answering the question, 'Where's Dad?' with, 'He's out the back, writing.'

A very special thanks to the incredible photographer James Penlidis, who generously allowed me to scour his archives to find photos of some of the contributors. Understandably, no one really had any photos of their bad gigs, so I decided instead to include shots from early in their careers. James has been photographing comedians for nearly 20 years and I am glad to give people the opportunity to see some of his excellent work. Thanks also to the other comedians who allowed me to use their photos here.

Thanks to all at The Five Mile Press especially Julia Taylor, Kay Scarlett, Shaun Jury, Phil Campbell, Juliet Chan, Nicole Ackland, Zoe Burdack, Kath de Reus, Alexandra Maramenides and Andrew Carroll, with a special mention to Stewart Clark. Thanks to the elusive Linda Funnell for once again doing a sterling job as my editor. I am sure I will meet you one day.

Thanks also to Janet McLeod and Peter Milne.

Thanks to Colin Lane and Frank Woodley for permission to use lyrics from 'Sonya'.

Thanks to George Smilovici for permission to use lyrics from 'I'm Tuff'.

ILLUSTRATION LIST

'Kiss Thiss' *(Rusty Berther)* 3
Sacred Wired Little Guys *(Rusty Berther)* 8
Jimeoin Jimmy James' first ever publicity shot *(James Penlidis)* 9
Russell Gilmore and Trev Mammulate – dunno where Glenn
 Rubins was *(James Penlidis)* 10
Bradley Cakes and Pasta the Juggler *(James Penlidis)* 11
'I've got a feeling, got a bit of an inkling, this is gonna be one of
 those days . . .' *(James Penlidis)* 17
Tripod in their younger days – that's Moby on the left
 (James Penlidis) 29
'Greeting cards – that's fascinating! Oh, I should introduce myself
 – Nicole Burchmore, pleased to meet you.' *(James Penlidis)* 31
Bruno Lucia as his alter ego 'Dino Valentino' – Hey, Dino, play that
 Sonya song! *(James Penlidis)* 42
So then he said, 'Are youse gonna sing that fucken Sonya
 song?' and I said, 'Give us a hundred bucks and we'll do it!'
 (Peter Milne) 45
Wil Anderson *(James Penlidis)* 53
Greg Fleet *(James Penlidis)* 62
'I'm Tuff! – most of the time!' *(George Smilovici)* 68
Tim Smith – one finger for each of his audience members
 (James Penlidis) 74
Andrew Goodone contemplating the 'good times'
 (James Penlidis) 77
Lawrence Mooney – what a nice looking young fellow!
 (James Penlidis) 92
I'm so glad I kept all of this memorabilia. I still can't believe I met
 Dr Kenneth Cooper! *(Rusty Berther)* 126

My hand-typed résumé that I used to join Actors Equity so I could meet Meryl Streep. Some of it is true *(Rusty Berther)*   135

Hey, Adam, whatever you do, don't drink what's in that glass *(Rich Hardcastle)*   146

We did around 20 spots on *Hey Hey It's Saturday* and this was a typical line-up *(Rusty Berther)*   152

Dave O'Neil living the dream. Is it hot in here, or is it just me? *(James Penlidis)*   159

Dave Callan. Even chicken wire wouldn't help at some gigs *(James Penlidis)*   163

Concert tickets *(Rusty Berther)*   168

Raymond J Bartholomew contemplating the intricacies of performing to Year 9 students *(James Penlidis)*   176

Concert passes (Rusty Berther)   184

Glenn Robbins as Uncle Arthur *(James Penlidis)*   190

Rusty and Sherry Sue. Sweet singing, good timing country duo *(Rusty Berther)*   193

Lano and Woodley's review *(Colin Lane)*   199

The line-up of the weekend's shows from 20 July 1990 at Le Joke, Collingwood *(Stef Torok)*   204

Harley Breen around the time of his wedding MD debut *(James Penlidis)*   210

Jodie J Hill obviously not affected by the sight of Whip's wang *(James Penlidis)*   214

Dave Hughes around the time of his first career-boosting trip to Edinburgh *(James Penlidis)*   221

Frank Woodley, Colin Lane and Scott Casley performing as the Found Objects *(James Penlidis)*   223

Andrew Goodone and Tim Smith as The Basters Theatre of Prague in happier times *(Andrew Goodone)*   226

The 3 Canadians – yes, there are four of them *(James Penlidis)*   238

Anthony Morgan, Peter Rowsthorn, Greg Fleet and Andrew Goodone in the 1980s *(James Penlidis)*   250